KATHARINE STEWART lives in Inverness. Born in 1914, she spent her early years in Musselburgh, and studied French at Edinburgh University. Then, during the war years, she worked for the Admiralty in London. She then moved to Abriachan, near Inverness, where she ran a croft and wrote documentaries for the BBC.

She has written numerous articles for various magazines, as well as several books. She was instrumental in setting up the museum at Abriachan. In April 2005 she received the Saltire Society Highland Branch Award for Contribution to the Understanding of Highland Culture, in recognition of her many works.

Women of the Highlands

KATHARINE STEWART

with a foreword by
Margaret Elphinstone

Luath Press Limited

EDINBURGH

www.luath.co.uk

To women everywhere,
those custodians of life

First Published 2006
This edition 2011
Reprinted 2013

ISBN: 978-1-906817-92-3

The paper used in this book is recyclable. It is made from
low chlorine pulps produced in a low energy, low emissions
manner from renewable forests.

MIX
Paper from
responsible sources
FSC
www.fsc.org   FSC® C007785

Printed and bound by
Bell & Bain Ltd., Glasgow

Typeset in 10.5 point Sabon by
3btype.com

Acknowledgements

MY VERY REAL THANKS go to Margaret Elphinstone for so kindly writing the foreword to this book.

My warm thanks go, as always, to the staffs of the Genealogical Department of the Highland Archives and to those of the Reference and Lending Departments of the Inverness Public Library, for their generous gifts of time and expertise in the provision of research material – books, records, papers, maps.

To my daughter Hilda and my granddaughter Fiona went the task of deciphering and computerising my script. Special thanks to them for their splendid work and blessings on them for not finding the task too tedious!

Contents

Chronology

c. 4000 BC	Bronze Age hunter-gatherers
c. 700 BC – 500 AD	Iron Age settlers
43 AD – 450 AD	Roman occupation
c. 455 AD	Brigid of Kildare born
c. 525 AD	Brigid, now St Bride, died
565 AD	St Columba arrives from Ireland
697 AD	Adamnan, Abbot of Iona, advocates exemption from military service for women
c. 800 AD	Norse Invasions
1224	Euphemia of Duffus Castle married
1314	Battle of Bannockburn
1513	Battle of Flodden
c. 1569	Mairi MacLeod born
1590	Katharine Ross and Hector Munro tried for witchcraft
1597	King James VI's *Daemonologie* published
1627	Magdalen Carnegie betrothed to the Earl of Montrose
1662	Isobel Gowdie convicted of witchcraft
1674	Mairi MacLeod died at Dunvegan
1689	Battle of Killiecrankie
1692	Massacre of Glencoe
1707	Union of Parliaments
1715, 1719 and 1745	Jacobite uprisings
1722	Flora MacDonald born
1727	Last judicial execution of witches
1746	Battle of Culloden
1749	Jane Maxwell, Duchess of Gordon, born
1755	Anne Grant of Laggan born
1775–1783	American War of Independence
1780s	Tartan becomes fashionable in London
1789	French Revolution
1790	Flora MacDonald died
1793–1815	Napoleonic Wars
1797	Elizabeth Grant of Rothiemurchus born
1803	*The Highlanders and other Poems* by Anne Grant published

1806	*Letters from the Mountains* by Anne Grant published
1808	*Memoirs of an American Lady* by Anne Grant published
1811	*Essays on the Superstitions of the Highlands* by Anne Grant published
1812	Duchess of Gordon died
1821	Màiri Mhór born
1823	Jemima Blackburn born
18th and 19th centuries	Emigration and Highland Clearances
1838	Anne Grant of Laggan died
1840	Frances Tolmie born
1843	Disruption in Church of Scotland
1848	*Phaeton* by Jemima Blackburn hung in the Royal Academy
1854	*Illustrations from Scripture by an Animal Painter with Notes by a Naturalist* by Jemima Blackburn published
1862	*Birds From Nature* by Jemima Blackburn published
1872	Education Act
1879	Edinburgh University admits women
1882	Battle of the Braes, Skye
	Elizabeth Grant of Rothiemurchus died
1886	Crofters Act
1887	Isabel Frances Grant born
1891	Màiri Mhór's poetry published
	Jemima Blackburn met Beatrix Potter
1895	*The Gesto Collection of Highland Music* ed. Dr Keith Norman MacDonald published
1898	Death of Màiri Mhór naw Oran
	A Highland Lady by Elizabeth Grant published
1899–1902	Boer War
1900	First volumes of the *Carmina Gadelica* by Alexander Carmichael published
1903	Margaret Fay Shaw born
1909	Jemima Blackburn died
1910	National Vigilance Committee set up to protect Highland girls working in cities

1911	*Journal of the Folk-Song Society* published Frances Tolmie's collection of Gaelic songs
1914–1918	First World War
1924	Frances Tolmie becomes honorary member of the Royal Celtic Society for services to Gaelic learning
1927	Frances Tolmie died
1930	Highland Exhibition held in Inverness
1939–1945	Second World War
1944	'Am Fasgadh' Folk Museum opened
c. 1950	Power is generated
1956	Dr Isabel Frances Grant received the MBE
1966	*Highland Folkways* by Isabel Frances Grant published
1981	Isle of Canna given to the National Trust for Scotland
1983	Dr Isabel Frances Grant died
c. 1990 on	Telecommunications develop
2004	Death of Margaret Fay Shaw

Foreword

WOMEN OF THE HIGHLANDS have always told their stories; their stories, legends, songs and charms have been handed down, in Gaelic, and later in English, through generations of Highland women, until the individual and specific merges into the shadow of the undocumented 'long-ago'. Katharine Stewart's latest book has the authority of being part of the living tradition it describes: a book about Highland women by a Highland woman, who is herself part of the seamless tradition. Like Elizabeth Grant of Rothiemurchus, Katharine Stewart writes about her own beloved country. Her anecdotes of individual women have an air of intimacy and understanding about her subjects that comes from belonging to the same world. She writes as if she knows them. At the same time, Elizabeth Grant in the nineteenth century, and Katharine Stewart in the twenty-first, bring to their subject the knowledge of a wider world, and the intellectual discipline acquired in a post-Enlightenment, literate, English-speaking Scotland. *Women of the Highlands* is the result of much research, and often the reader has a sense of a shadowy half-known tale brought into the light of day, and carefully examined from all angles. How many readers will know, for example, the full story of Flora MacDonald, whose reluctant aid to a fleeing prince was just one brief incident in a life shaped by the changes that were to alter the eighteenth century Highland world beyond recognition: rebellion, clearances, agricultural improvement, emigration and colonial wars? Throughout the book respect for legend goes hand in hand with a meticulous regard for fact, and the reader is made to see that both kinds of truth are necessary to do full justice to the story of the women of the Highlands.

In some respects women's lives differ greatly from one another according to historical time and individual circumstance. In other ways women's lives do not alter, in so far as they are shaped by the very fact of being female, by marriage, childbirth, family, personal tragedy, and the proverbial women's work which, however easy or hard it may be in any given situation, is never, and never will be, done. *Women of the Highlands* moves to and fro from the general to the particular, its structure a clear acknowledgement of the fact that the vast majority of women have no memorial. Whole chapters are dedicated to telling how ordinary women lived and died, from Celtic to contemporary times. In these sections there is a strong sense of how the past lives on today. Marriage, pregnancy, childbirth, and the bond with the land are themes that do not die, however much history sweeps over them. At times Highland history has been peculiarly harsh. The story of Highland women is necessarily one of loss and suffering as well as celebration. The evil is plainly told here as well as the good, notably some of the horrific history of the Scottish witch trials, including the notorious trial of Isobel Gowdie, still remembered around Auldearn today. Later on we see the terrible effects of the Clearances on Highland society as a whole, and how they affected the recorded lives of individual women.

Lament goes hand in hand with celebration: the lyrical description of life at the shielings, for example, breathes life into the ruins one sees so often at the top of a remote glen or on a high hillside. The reader feels both enrichment and loss at the same time, which is very much like listening to Highland song. Weddings, births, farming customs: so much has gone, and yet it's good to be aware of what remains, often in attenuated rituals or small customs that many readers will have experienced in their own lives today.

Naturally several of the women celebrated in the book are singers, because that is the major form of expression in Gaelic cultures, and the text echoes the notes sounded by some of its women characters. Generations of unnamed women sang waulking songs, lullabies and laments. The names of a few live on, like Màiri MacLeod and, later, Màiri Mhór 'the bard of the Land Reform Movement', who was both singer and political activist (as well as nurse and obstetrician). After suffering unjust imprisonment, she went on to compose many songs, and to fight for the reforms that successfully led to the Crofters' Act in 1886. For bards, poets and writers, Highland life at all levels meant that art was one aspect of a busy practical life.

The overriding impression of Katharine Stewart's book is its richness of texture. Women of the Highlands have led full, varied lives, sometimes within the confines of a small island, sometimes spanning countries and continents. Recorded lives are necessarily biased in favour of the aristocracy, but this book redresses that imbalance by focussing on the ways in which individual women are part of a larger, seamless tradition of women's tasks and arts. The vignettes of individual lives show women of talent, courage and resource, who are the shapers of history as well as its victims. They suffer the violence and cruelty which have played too large a part in Highland history, but here we also see them as survivors, embodying and celebrating a living tradition. Because of their activities over the centuries, many good things have come to pass. A few heroic deeds have become part of recorded history. The abiding sense of this book is of a more wide-ranging heroism, of the countless women of the Highlands who made life rich in the fullest sense of the word, often in the poorest of circumstances, and managed not only to survive, but to protest against injustice, record their histories, emigrate, learn new skills, sing, write, paint... to celebrate who they were and where they belonged, whatever the odds.

Margaret Elphinstone

Introduction

Women of the Highlands

WOMEN, PEOPLE OF the allegedly weaker sex, have tended to occupy but little space in the story of their country. Kings and warriors, bishops and barons, speculators and improvers, their feats and follies shaped the land.

It was, nevertheless, to the women who bore and reared them, that these men owed their strength of body and mind, to those women who watched and waited, counselled or encouraged. In a recent widespread poll it was reckoned that the most valued word in the language, in any language, was 'mother'. The instinct of childless women was, and often is, to 'mother' others or causes in which they believe.

It was always the women who were closest to the land on which they lived, especially those high lands which were nearer to the sun but which yet bore hard on human life, with sudden storm, darkness among the rocks, quick spate in the quiet burns. But to those with the soft tread, the quick eye and the lively mind land, however remote from habitation, yielded sustenance and healing. The machair, that coastal meadowland in the Islands, bore a rich profusion of plant life. On the steepest hillside grew juniper and cranberry, which later became badges of the clans. In sheltered hollows berries and nuts abounded, to make squirrel-like provision for the winter days.

Men were the hunters, women the gatherers, moving quietly among the treasures, storing up knowledge to pass on to the generation ahead. It was a long process of trial and error, finding what nourished and what healed.

This was one of the first skills acquired by women as they struggled to keep their families fit and able. We still benefit from the discoveries they made as they roamed the moors and forests. Berried fruit, nuts, garlic, thyme, aspirin (from meadowsweet) are all known to keep us in good health today. Throughout passages of terror and distress, as well as in the blessed times of calm, women were working at their steady tasks – protecting the children, safeguarding crops and animals. Always on the side of life.

As their long sustained strength came to be recognised so they came to stand tall alongside the men, not in battle order, but, hopefully, in the patient pursuit of peace.

CHAPTER I

Early Women – Celtic Times

IN CELTIC SOCIETY IN the first centuries AD women were held in high regard. Their social status was quite remarkable. They could become chiefs and take prominent roles in political, religious and artistic life; judges, law-givers and bards. They could choose their marriage partners and could divorce them if maltreated, having the right to claim damages. Their dowry remained their property. In Britain matri-linear succession to kingship was the rule until the 9th century.

In pre-Christian times Celtic female deities were all in the form of an earth-mother. Lucius Apuleius, a Roman writer of the 2nd century, observing this, had a poem:

I am she
That is the natural
Mother of all things,
Mistress and governess
Of all the elements
The initial progeny of worlds
Chief of the powers divine
Queen of all that are in hell
The principal of them
That dwell in heaven
Manifested alone
And understood form
Of all the gods and goddesses.

The belief in a goddess of creation was deep-rooted in many parts of the world.

The Celtic people lived in close-knit units known as kins, or families of several generations. They shared the responsibilities of family life, the raising of children and so on. Care of the sick was a bounden duty in what was almost a welfare state.

Fostering was an important common practice. The foster parents would train the children entrusted to them from an early age in adult skills. The boy would be returned to his biological parents at the age of 17, the girl at 14. The bond between foster-parents and children and particularly between foster-brothers, was very strong and enduring. The fostering habit persisted until the 19th century. The land was held in common by the kin. This idea of kin was to continue through the ages and is still evident today, in the closeness of family ties among the people of the Highlands.

It is to the Roman writers of the early centuries that we owe our knowledge of the Celtic peoples, those of Gaul and later of Britain, of themselves and their way of life. Ptolemy wrote down the names of the tribes in north Britain. Caesar and Tacitus also refer to the ways of the people, allowing us to piece together a view of what these might have been.

We even have a picture of their personal lives, their fastidious insistence on cleanliness, on frequent bathing and on neatness of apparel. Their skills in working metals enabled the casting of elaborate brooches, torcs (neck-bands) and armlets worn by both men and women. Both sexes also wore the same kind of woven clothing.

In appearance the Celts are described as tall, muscled and white of skin. They are also said to be loud-mouthed and boastful. The Romans certainly found them to be a formidable enemy. Amminiamus Marcellinus, writing during the 4th century, draws an unforgettable picture of the Gaulish women warriors:

Nearly all the Gauls are of a lofty stature, fair and of

ruddy complexion, terrible from the sternness of their eyes, very quarrelsome and of great pride and insolence. A whole troop of foreigners would not be able to withstand a single Gaul if he called his wife to his assistance, who is usually very strong and with blue eyes; especially when, stretching her neck, gnashing her teeth and brandishing her sallow arms of enormous size, she begins to strike blows mingled with kicks, as if they were so many missiles sent from the string of a catapult. The voices of these women are formidable and threatening, even when they are not angry but being friendly. But all the Celtic women with equal care keep neat and clean and in some areas no woman can be seen, be she never so poor, in soiled or ragged clothing.

Later, in 697 AD, Adamnan, Abbot of Iona, in his 'Laws of the Innocents' was to advocate exemption from military activity for women and to pass Acts raising their status by imposing stiff penalties for assaults. Children were also to be protected.

Scáthach

Scáthach, a woman warrior, ran a martial arts academy in Skye. Whether or not she is the stuff of legend, someone of her ilk must surely have existed. Her castle of Sgiathanach later became a Macleod stronghold and can still be seen and the ruins visited.

Boudicca

One woman warrior of whose existence we are sure is Boudicca of the Iceni tribe in Britain, who lived in the 1st century AD. Tacitus, the Roman historian, quotes her as saying:

I take the field like the ordinary citizen among you to assert the cause of liberty, to seek justice for my body scarred with the Roman lash and to avenge my raped daughters.

She gathered several tribes to join her and inflicted much damage on the Roman armies, driving her war chariot fearlessly among them, her red hair streaming in the wind, until eventually suffering defeat. Her end is not known. Did she die of illness? Did she take poison to avoid being taken into slavery? Her burial is not recorded.

St Bride

With the coming of Christianity among the Celtic people a new world opened up in which women would take an important place – the world of the Church. Here we have the record of another early Celtic woman, Brigid of Kildare. She lived in Ireland c455–525 AD and was to become revered as 'Mary of the Gaels'. She was born in County Down and named for Brigid, the goddess of fertility and of healing, poetry and fire. Her father was a Druid, so she was brought up steeped in Druidism. She became a ban-drui, or female Druid, but at an early age she converted to Christianity, studying under a bishop. When she began giving away her father's goods, including his sword, to the needy he became alarmed and placed her as bond-servant to the King of Leinster, with a view to his marrying her. But she would have none of this, took a vow of chastity and made off to study under Mel, Bishop of Armagh. He ordained her as a priest. Later she was to become a bishop. Clearly her abilities were remarkable. How today's authorities would view her career is a matter of speculation.

Brigid set up a Christian community at Drumcree, under the

shadow of a huge oak, the tree that was sacred to the Druids. Her next foundation at Kildare, on the Curragh, also had a connection to the oak; the name means 'church of the oaks'. This was a mixed community, with men and women living and worshipping together as equals. It was a simple little monastery: a few small dwelling-huts and oratories. But learning was going on there, people were being taught to read and to chant. Brigid became its abbess.

Sexual relationships in Celtic society were based on a realistic acceptance of the facts of life – love of one of the opposite or the same sex, jealousy, cruelty, divorce, multiple partners. The clergy at this time were generally non-celibate. Mixed communities were common, influenced by the same Celtic ideas. Hilda, the Abbess of Whitby, ran a community in the 7th century which included the poet Caedmon.

In remembrance of the goddess of fire, the fire at Brigid's community was never allowed to go out. In a 'Smooring Blessing' one of the many collected by Alexander Carmichael in the 19th century, we find the lines:

I will smoor the hearth
As Mary would smoor,
The encompassment of Bride and of Mary
On the fire and on the floor
And on the household all.

To 'smoor' meant to smother the flames with ash, so that they could be blown into life in the morning. The little foundation at Kildare eventually became one of the great Irish monastic institutions.

Brigid of Kildare was renowned over the Celtic world and eventually sainthood was conferred upon her and she became

known as Saint Bride. Her 'day' in the calendar is 1 February, the 'birthday' of the year, the time when ewes come into milk, that valued sustenance of the people. So St Bride keeps contact with the essential reality of the world. In the Highlands of Scotland many wells, sources of healing and many churches are dedicated to her. In myth she became known as the midwife of the Virgin Mary and even the foster-mother of Christ.

Women in Celtic society certainly had a higher status than their counterparts in Rome or Athens where repressive male dominance kept them in subordinate roles. Norse women coming into the Highlands and the islands during Viking times, i.e. the 8th and 9th centuries AD, also had less freedom than their Celtic contemporaries, their role being more specifically a domestic one. Several did however acquire fame for their seamanship on voyages of exploration. With gradual integration through inter-marriage they soon adopted the status of the women around them.

In his book *The Ancient World of the Celts* Peter Beresford Ellis tells us: 'a unique piece of feminist literature' emerges from 12th century Ireland in the form of *Bauschenaus* – a book on the genealogies of leading women. In fact this could be claimed as the first European book about women in their own right.

Mediaeval Times – Women of the Castles

IN MEDIAEVAL TIMES, the pattern of life began to change. Power was now vested in the king rather than shared among the kins or tribes, with charters of land granted to the chiefs of what were to become clans. The structure of the erstwhile tribe had become hierarchical.

As the demand for land became competitive the chief required military support from the lower orders as a form of rental for their holdings. As he was frequently feuding with other equally pugnacious or territorial chiefs, his followers were often on active service. At these times work on the land and the handling of stock were all done by women. Many were widowed, for clan battles were fierce, but some provision was made for women thus left. Meanwhile other ways of acquiring territory were being exploited by some chiefs – the marrying-off, often at a very early age, of their daughters to the sons of other chiefs.

Euphemia of Duffus Castle

Euphemia, daughter of Farquhar MacTaggart, the lay Abbot of Applecross, on the north-west coast, had an 'arranged marriage' to Walter, grandson of Freskin the Fleming, an incoming feudal knight who had been given the lands of Duffus in Moray by King David I.

She was baptised Eighrig, Gaelic being the tongue of all her people in Applecross. Her upbringing had been that of the daughter of a land-owning farmer: probably living in quite a modest house, with walls of turf and a cruck-beamed roof, thatched with heather. Much of her time would have been spent out of doors, riding her pony, helping with tasks such as fetching water from the well, gathering herbs, stacking peat. She would also have learnt to churn, to spin wool and flax, to knit, to embroider. Though there was no formal schooling for girls at that time, she might well have shared in the reading lessons her brother William would have been given by the local priest. In the long winter evenings, at the ceilidh, she would listen to the stories of her ancestors' deeds and join in the singing of the lovely songs of Gaeldom. Then, in 1215, her father announced that, in return for services to King Alexander, he had been given land at Delny in Easter Ross, and that he and the family would be going there to claim this inheritance. So, after a long and arduous cross-country journey, they took up residence in this flat, strange land.

It was not long before Farquhar's thoughts turned to the marrying of his daughter. The marriages of people of rank were extremely serious affairs. The young couple could have been betrothed, perhaps hand-fasted, in front of witnesses, by the age of 7, the marriage then solemnised when the girl reached the age of 12, and the boy the age of 14. This was not the case for Eighrig of course, she would have been about 14 at the time of her marriage.

The terms of the bride's dowry were always carefully drawn up. In Eighrig's case land was ceded to her husband, in return for 'services' to himself and to the king and for 'one pound of pepper on the feast of St Martin'. Pepper was valued for its use in concealing the smell of tainted meat.

After the church wedding celebrations would go on for at least a week, with much feasting, drinking, falconry, archery, dancing, romancing.

Then, in 1224, Eighrig went to live in her married home at

Duffus Castle, a huge, stone-built, bleak motte-and-bailey place. Much of it still stands today, a symbol of power and authority. Here, her name changed to Euphemia, the young bride had to adapt to life in the Norman style, to perfect her English and to learn French. She, who had been skilled in all the domestic arts since childhood in Applecross, came quite quickly to manage the household affairs of the place she was to call home. With her husband often away, involved in political manoeuvring, combat, visits overseas, as were many husbands of the elite, Euphemia also had to learn the laws concerning the administration of the estate, the appointment and dismissal of servants, and matters concerning the Church. There was also the entertainment of important guests. Some women entered into 'affairs' to promote their husband's interests. There is no record of this in Euphemia's case.

All of these duties she undertook while, over the years, suffering several stillbirths, infant deaths and thwarted pregnancies. At last a son was born successfully whom she named Freskin, in honour of her husband's family, so she mothered an heir. Whether love entered her relationship with her husband is not known, but they did not divorce, as in certain circumstances was permissible.

Walter died in 1262. The following year Euphemia made over her dowry lands to the Church. Her death is not recorded. She lived, and died, a woman of her time, of her station, like so many women subject to the will of the male members of her family – father, husband, son – yet creating for themselves a place of vital importance in the furthering of their adopted lineage.

Magdalen Carnegie

In 1627 Magdalen Carnegie was betrothed at age 14 to James Graham, Earl of Montrose, who was 16. A year later they were married. This was politically an astute move on her father's part, to which Magdalen had had to agree in order to please him, though she was actually in love with another. Her life consisted mostly in holding the fort while her husband was away fighting on one side or the other. She hated warfare, the killing and the maiming. Her first-born son was taken away by his father to join in the fighting, and died young. Heart-broken, she succumbed to illness and died at an early age.

These arranged marriages were many and continue today. They account for the pattern of land ownership in the Highlands as we know it, with estates merging.

CHAPTER 3

Mediaeval Times –
Women of the Settlements

WHILE THE WOMEN OF the castles pursued their busy lives, with times of festivity and of stress, the women outwith the castle walls, in the wider countryside, led lives of simple austerity with stresses of a different kind. They had their times of festivity too. These were associated with the seasons and with the basic elements that determined their prosperity, their very hold on life. Being devoutly Christian and, especially in the islands, followers of the Celtic Christian tradition of Saint Columba, they recognised the saints. As we have seen, St Bride was hallowed on 1 February, the birthday of spring; Beltane, a hang-over from pre-Christian sun-worshipping times, was celebrated in May when cattle were taken to pasture; St Martin in September with horse-racing; Samhain, our Halloween, when winter returned and winter stores were secured. Euphemia, remembering Applecross, would have recognised their way of living. As in her case, the women of the townships, as the settlements were called, had often to cope with all the work of their holdings, when their men were away fighting for their chief, or off on long hunting trips to provide food for their families. A woman left on her own did receive some help from the chief, but the greatest practical help came from members of the community. Her ploughing would be done, her fuel provided. This communal care for the deprived is still given today, as neighbours rally to help a widow.

In May when the cattle were taken up to the high pastures, it was the women who went with them, along with the girls, and a few boys as herds. Some horses and a few sheep and goats were often taken up, along with the cattle, so there was plenty for the boys to do.

The men would have gone up a few days beforehand to repair the small huts at the shieling in which the women and the young people would live. There would be several of these, one with a fire for the cooking, one with shelves for the milk vessels.

On the day of the 'big flitting' there would be great excitement – dogs barking, cattle lowing, children laughing and shouting, the women casting anxious glances at the loaded carts and panniers, making sure everything was there – milk vessels, butter churns, cheese presses, pots, pans, meal-bags, a salt box, spinning-wheels, spindles, flax, wool, blankets and clothing.

On the eve of departure a simple meal was taken in common, with a blessing invoked in song on the cattle to ensure their well-being.

Alexander Carmichael found this one, known as 'Columba's Herding':

> May the herding of Columba
> Encompass you going and returning
> Encompass you on strath and on ridge
> And on the edge of each rough region.
> May it keep you from pit and from mire
> Keep you from hill and from crag
> Keep you from loch and from downfall
> Each evening and each darkling.
> The peace of Columba be yours on the grazing
> The peace of Bridget be yours in the grazing
> The peace of Mary be yours in the grazing
> And may you return home safe-guarded.

The trek to shieling grounds would take the best part of a day. The men would have left some dry peats for the fire and heather for bedding.

As soon as the unloading was done it was time for the milking, on the green outside the dwellings. Sometimes the cow's back legs would be tied together to keep her steady after the excitement of the journey. The girls would have favourites among the cows, giving them names, knowing their individual ways, singing to them as they milked:

Lovely black cow, pride of the shieling,
First cow of the byre, choice mother of calves.
Wisps of straw round the cows of the townships
A shackle of silk on my heifer beloved
Ho, my heifer, ho my gentle heifer.

Goats would be milked too, and sometimes the few sheep which had been taken up. Their milk made excellent cheese.

Next day the dairying would begin. Large quantities of superb butter and cheese would be made. Some would be sent down to the men at home, some preserved in kegs buried in the peat. A form of milk shake was made by frothing up a cupful of milk with a special little plunger. A favourite dish was curds, and the whey was also drunk.

Life at the shielings was a busy time. As well as the dairying much spinning was done, of wool and of flax. Lichens and roots had to be gathered for dyeing the wool.

The boys, as well as herding the cattle, would do some wood-carving, making spoons, spirtles, or milk-whisks with a sharp knife. They would also provide for the larder, with a rabbit snared or trout guddled from the burn. In the long evenings they would raise a tune on a whistle for some dancing on the green. As the herd-boys cast eyes at the dairy-maids, charming love-songs were sung or even composed on the spot:

> Brown-haired girl I would choose you
> Ho-ro, you would be my choice.
> Brown-haired girl I would choose you
> For sweetness and for beauty.
> Brown-haired girl of the fold
> Young did I give you my devotion.
> No other shall take you from me
> Unless he wins you with gold.

While life at the shielings was going busily and happily along, the men back at the townships were also busy and no doubt enjoying many a ceilidh together, with a smoke and a dram in the evenings. Some would take the opportunity to re-thatch the house. Some would be making brogues for the winter, or getting on with weaving or tailoring, if they were so skilled.

Towards the end of the summer, when the hill grass was getting past its best there would be a move home from the shielings, the cattle fat and glossy, the boys and girls similarly robust, thriving on the hill air and the hill food. Good stocks of butter and cheese and good lengths of woollen and linen fabric were packed into carts. All the produce of the summer days in the hills would help to see the families through the winter ahead.

There was great rejoicing as the home-coming was celebrated, husbands and wives reunited and all the news exchanged. In wilder times a hunting party would sometimes descend on a shieling, carrying off the produce and assaulting the girls. The women had to struggle in defence of their little colony.

The sojourn at the shielings, with the women in charge, was a valuable part of the pattern of the year, beneficial in every way. Sadly, little trace can now be found of the places that were once so full of life. The small dwellings have weathered away, though patches of bright green sward still mark the spots where the cattle grazed.

And the songs remain.

Brown-haired lass of the shieling
I would surely sit with you
On the top of the high hills
And on the shieling of the hillock!

Snug at a winter ceilidh, the singing can bring back all the magic of the long summer days.

Once settled in their homes again it was back to the routine work of the holdings, the women taking part in all of it, even an autumn ploughing, certainly the harrowing, harnessed to the harrows like a horse. And they would carry the peat from the moor and the seaweed from the shore, often working a spindle while they walked. The work was hard beyond our imagining today. But there were songs to help on every kind of job.

CHAPTER 4

Work Songs and Incantations

SONGS FOR THE MEN needed strong beats and rhythms for the communal effort of rowing or reaping. For the women's more solitary occupations – milking, churning, spinning, weaving, working the quern, or hand-mill – less emphatic rhythms were needed, though they were timed to fit the movements involved.

A churning song, sung watching the milk turn into butter, has almost incantatory verses:

> Come thou churn come
> Come thou churn come
> The churning made of Mary
> In the fastness of the glen
> To decrease her milk
> To increase her butter,
> Buttermilk to wrist
> Butter to elbow
> Come thou churn come
> Come thou churn come.

Querning, a way of grinding corn, was usually done by two women sitting on the ground, between them two flat stones, one on top of the other. The upper stone had a wooden handle which the women could grasp, one to push the stone, the other to pull, in a rotatory movement, as the grain was fed in. The stones were heavy and it was a monotonous task. A song was essential to keep the work going on.

One such is from the island of Barra:

Quern, quern, grind
Quern, quern, grind,
Old woman grind the quern
And you shall have the quern bannock
I will not grind it indeed
That does not bestir me.

To quicken the movement and mill the grain more finely the second
verse changed:

Quern, quern, grind,
Quern, quern, grind.
Old woman grind the quern
And you shall have the good man's son.
 I will grind and feed.
I will feed the quern and grind!

If singing a child to sleep is considered labour, there were certainly
many lovely Gaelic lullabies:

The nest of the laverock
Is in the track of Dubhag,
My little one will sleep and he shall have the bird
The nest of the mavis
Is in the bonnie copse
My little one will sleep and he shall have the bird
The nest of the curlew
Is in the bubbling peat-moss
My little one will sleep and he shall have the bird.

At a time of death the 'keening' or dirge was sung by a woman. And a woman, specially employed as a mourning woman, sang the 'coronach', extolling the virtues of the deceased, on the way to the graveyard.

Perhaps the most common labour song was that sung at the 'waulking', that is, the shrinking of the newly woven cloth. This was work undertaken by women on their own, with men excluded. And they enjoyed it! A group of about a dozen women would sit round a long board, often a door taken off its hinges for the occasion. The cloth which had been soaking in a tub, most often of urine, would be laid on the board, gripped by the women and passed sun-wise from hand to hand, with a hearty thump. The leading woman would start the song, singing the first verse solo, the others joining in the chorus. Often it was a satirical song, poking fun at men and their ways. The rhythm was like an African drum-beat and made for excitement in the work. Sometimes an extra beat would add pith to the performance and an impromptu verse would record some recent event in the community. As the cloth got drier and lighter the tempo increased, rising almost to a frenzy. No man would dare to venture on the scene!

In very old times the waulking was done with the feet, the women sitting on the ground, making kicking movements. This must have been less conducive to singing, even of satirical songs.

Some women still sing the old waulking songs, for pleasure, sitting round the room, holding a piece of cloth and moving it to the rhythm of the song. These songs, often spontaneously created, full of passion and humour, are quite unique, found only in the culture of the Hebrides.

In spite of all the banter and the fun of being on their own the women cherished their men. Love songs tell of this. Often they are sad because partings were many, as were losses from fighting or drowning. But the words ring true and the melodies are perfect. These came naturally to a people with eyes and ears alive to the living world around them. It is said that the sounds of the oyster-catcher, Brigid's bird, piping on the sands inspired the melody for a song of love. The surge of the sea, the soft wind through the birch leaves in summer, a sudden dazzle of snow, the roar of the stags in autumn, all these natural sounds and sights would have fed the imaginations of people who had time to heed them.

Eriskay Love Lilt

When I'm lonely, dear white heart
Black the night, or wild the sea
By love's light my foot finds
The old pathway to thee.
Thou'rt the music of my heart,
Harp of joy and moon of guidance
Strength and light thou'rt to me,
Sad am I without thee.

Each small daily task had its own ritual accompaniment of poem or song. Every poem was a song to the Gaels. The kindling of the fire in the morning and the 'smooring' in the evening were acts of vital importance, for fire meant life; so each had their own incantation. The washing of shirts, the baking of oaten cakes, all the activities needed to sustain life, the soothing away of pain, the healing of wounds, these carried their own songs.

The mother had a blessing for her son leaving home:

The keeping of God upon thee in every pass,
The shielding of Christ upon thee in every path
The bathing of spirit upon thee in every stream
In every land and sea thou goest.

These songs and incantations were handed down, in the oral tradition over the ages. Many of them were collected by Alexander Carmichael, the Excise officer, whose work took him to many parts of the Highlands and the Islands. It was mostly the women who gave him the songs, the blessings, the charms, the incantations. He has recorded many of their names in the notes to the volumes of his collected work – *Carmina Gadelica*. The women would sing the poem, he would write it down in Gaelic, then later translate it into English. He was a native Gaelic speaker from the island of Lismore.

Thus, he tells us that 'A Fairy Song' was given to him by a 'black-haired, fine-featured intelligent woman in Mingulay. The woman first sang this very sweetly and then dictated it with great intelligence.'

A Fairy Song

'Tis I that am pained
For the woman that was in Dùn Trò
Where I lost my brothers
And my three young babes
My father and my mother
Are laid under the sod
Aparan duibh o hi ho
Ro hu ill o ho.

'The Fairy Lover' was sung by 'a woman of 70 or 80, above middle height, mild, dignified and vivacious when speaking. Her figure and complexion were such as a court lady might envy'. She had never been out of her native South Uist and had never heard a word of English.

The Fairy Lover

What, my love, shall I do with thee?
What food and clothing give to thee?
Alas and alas now for myself!
Thou hast broken the cockles of my heart!

I'll carry thee home to the fairy bower,
Where thou shall have food in plenty,
Meal and milk, cream and butter,
And the milking of the cow-folds.

The Carlin of Beinn Bhreac

The Carlin of Beinn Bhreac ho,
Bhreac ho, Bhreac ho
The Carlin of Beinn Bhreac ho,
The tall carlin of the mountain spring.

I would not let my herd of deer,
My herd of deer, my herd of deer,
I would not let my herd of deer
Go nibble the grey shells of the shore.

I am a carlin ranging bens,
Ranging bens, ranging bens,
I am a carlin ranging bens
Trying to see the best glen.

The wonderful woman who sang this song and many others was
Mary Macrae, in her 99th year. From Isobel MacNeill, cottar, of
Barra, came 'The New Moon' and 'The White Moon of the Night'.

The New Moon

I am lifting to thee my hands,
I am bowing to thee my head,
I am giving thee my love
Thou glorious jewel of all the ages.

I am raising to thee my eye,
I am bending to thee my head,
I am offering to thee my love,
Thou new moon of all the ages!

From Mary MacRae of Harris came a 'Cattle Croon'. From Peggy McCormack of South Uist a 'Night Prayer'. From Barbara MacPhee, cottar, of Drimsdale, Uist, a 'Death Prayer'. From Mary MacNeill of Barra, 'My Brown Cow,' sung to make the cow give milk. It's good that we have a record of these, and many more, women of the islands.

CHAPTER 5

Mairi MacLeod (*c.*1569 – *c.*1674) – Bard

A WOMAN POET OR bard of the seventeenth century has left a record of her name, her life and some of her poems. She was Mairi nighean Alasdair ruadh, Mairi daughter of red-haired Alasdair MacLeod, born in 1569 on the Isle of Harris. As a young woman she worked as a nanny to the MacLeod household at Dunvegan, whither she had moved. In later life her poetic talent emerged and she composed many songs and poems in praise of the MacLeods.

A poem of hers which has survived is 'Part of a dirge on the death of a beloved chieftan, Sir Norman MacLeod of Berneray', translated by J. Carmichael Watson.

In thee would be found dignity and
blitheness, in the hour of judgement.
Thou wouldst solve the case, not with
sullenness or anger, but courtly, orderly, with reason.

Thou wast the tranquillity of friends at
times of homecoming, when men
drank deep without discord or quarrel,
and thou didst love to have by thee
tellers of a rare and pleasing tale.
Often did friends wend to thy glorious
fortress, that was blithe and welcoming,
festive and stately, without turbulence
or arrogance, where the needy was not denied his due.

This dirge is typical of the praise-poetry which was composed for chiefs during their life-time.

Mairi was quite a forceful character, fond of her dram and her pinch of snuff. Discarding some of the traditional bardic rules, she developed her own style of expression: using words full of praise for the family but being, perhaps, over-liberal in her description of the extravagant life-style of those at Dunvegan castle. Her compositions causing displeasure to the chief, she was banished to the isle of Mull.

In her exile she continued to compose. Perhaps her best known poem 'Luinneag Mhicleoid' – 'MacLeod's Song' – came from her lonely years.

The chief then relented and she was allowed to return on condition that she did not express herself as before. Sadly, many of her poems have been lost, or are not ascribed to her.

Mairi died at Dunvegan castle in 1674, aged 105. Her remains were ferried over to the church at Rodil, in Harris, where many MacLeod chiefs were buried. It is said that she asked to be interred face down, so that her tongue, which had uttered lies, would not point to heaven. So here she lies at peace, under the floor of this beautiful church, below the window in the south transept.

CHAPTER 6

Marriage Customs

A WEDDING WAS AN occasion for a whole community to rejoice. A wedding meant life, meant the future. It was best to marry on a waxing moon and preferably on a Friday, the day called for Freya, the Norse goddess of love.

In some cases the church wedding might have been preceded by a 'hand-fast' union, when a couple would link hands in a hollowed-out stone and, in the presence of witnesses, declare themselves married for a year and a day. If, after that time, they wished to continue their life together they would seek a blessing on this union or they could separate without malice.

The usual church marriage would have come about after a 'reitach', or form of betrothal. Following this custom the young man would have gone with a friend to the house of the girl he wished to marry, to ask her father's consent to the marriage.

Over a dram or two the friend would extol the virtues of the aspirant while the girl waited in another room. When the father had been suitably impressed, she would be summoned and, after she had declared her willingness to marry her suitor, the couple would share a dram from the same glass.

Another somewhat unusual pre-nuptial custom was that known as 'bundling.' The young couple would share a bed, fully clothed, sometimes with a bolster between them, spending the night talking of their plans for the future, their hopes, their fears, getting to know each other.

On the morning of the wedding day a white flag, usually a tablecloth, would be flown from the chimney of the bride's house.

The company – bride, family and friends – would walk in procession to the church, pipes playing, perhaps a gun-shot or two to ward off any lurking evil spirits. Guests from far and wide would be gathering by the door.

After the service there would be a huge meal in the barn, the only place big enough to hold the crowd. Lots of food would have been brought in by neighbours – chicken, potatoes, cheese, eggs, bannocks, butter, food of all kinds, saved over days. It would be a noisy meal, with lots of gossip, teasing, and banter. When appetites were satisfied the makeshift tables would be packed away and the floor cleared for dancing. Fiddle music was the best to get the feet moving and the accordion backed it up.

The young married couple had to endure many pranks before they could get away on their own. In the morning the girl's virginal head-band (the snood) would be replaced by the white head-covering of the married woman (the mutch). The festivities would go on for several days, till the food and drink ran out or the guests succumbed to exhaustion.

Then life for the newly weds began in earnest. They would receive gifts from neighbours to help them set up home – a bag of seed oats or potatoes, a load of dung or peats, a coop of chickens, some chairs or blankets. It was also the custom for them to go visiting more distant friends or relatives, looking for gifts.

The young bride would start her new life happy in the assurance that she and her husband had the support of the community. Should mischance such as a drowning at sea leave her a widow she knew that she need not fear destitution. In the upper échelons of society, in the castles, widowed, unmarried or handicapped women often went to live and work in convents. In the townships they were accepted as part of the community.

'Natural' children, those born outwith the legitimate family, were often numerous in courtly circles, where they could be adequately provided for. Foster children were accepted gladly by the lower orders, forging a link, as we have seen, with the clan chief.

Formal divorce did not occur among the poor, where there was little question of the partition of assets. Separations there may have been, in extreme circumstances of cruelty or dislike, but the close link between man and wife was essential in the ordering of daily life.

The young wife who had acquired all the skills, domestic and outdoor, necessary for her calling knew innately her worth as partner; workmate as well as lover and future mother. She could face the world with equanimity.

CHAPTER 7

Childbirth

CHILDBIRTH IS SURELY a most traumatic time in any woman's life. Small wonder then, that many customs and ceremonies have grown around it. Some are extant today, as echoes of those former times.

For Highland women in ages past, many pregnancies were the norm, as infant mortality came about quite frequently and children were prized. Conception would have been encouraged by the woman walking three times, sunwise (east to west), round a certain well before drinking the water. Rocking an empty cradle also helped.

St Bride, the goddess of childbirth who, it was believed, helped at the birth of Jesus, would have been invoked. And magic would not be far away, as the woman in labour clutched rowan berries to ease the pain.

Once the baby was born he or she was handed back and forth three times across the central fire, as fire protected against evil. Then it was carried three times, sunwise, round those present.

The great fear, in those old days, was that the 'fairies' would carry the child away, leaving a 'changeling' in its place. This fear must have originated in the fact that sometimes new-born infants were indeed stolen by people needing to build up the strength of another community. To put it down to the fairies was perhaps a form of propitiation.

At any rate, all known precautions against harm by the fairy folk were taken. An object made of iron, even a nail, would be placed under the mother's bed, for iron was a sure protection. The cradle was made of one of the sacred woods – elder, rowan, oak

– held together with iron nails. A borrowed cradle was preferred. In Christian times the father's dirk was sometimes placed in the cradle, the handle representing the cross. An object made of iron, which would jangle, was hung across the cradle. Fairies beware!

Even today, the baby's cot or pram is not put in place until after the birth. Providence must not be tempted!

A tiny spoonful of butter or a minute pinch of salt was often placed in the new-born baby's mouth. Thomas Pennant, who travelled the Highlands and Islands in the late 18th century, reported in 1772:

> [a nurse puts] the end of a green stick of ash into the fire and while it is burning receives into a spoon the sap or juice which oozes out of the other end and administers this as the first spoonful of liquor to the new-born babe.

The ash, with its deep roots and tall trunk, was a prized tree said to be a link between heaven and earth.

The baby was baptized as soon as possible after the birth. The cleric often had to travel a long distance. Meanwhile the woman attending the mother would give the infant a 'birth baptism' by putting three small drops of water on the tiny forehead – in the name of the Father, the Son and the Spirit. When bathing the baby she would sing 'a prayer of baptism – nine little wavelets of grace to thee' as recorded by Alexander Carmichael. The clerical baptism would take place a week or so later, when a gathering of family members and friends would attend and the baby would be passed round them, sunwise, as each expressed a wish for the child's future. Occasionally, a baby would be taken to the blacksmith for an 'owre iron' christening, just to make sure those fairies were kept at bay!

Then it was time to 'wet the baby's head' with a dram for the men and a cup of tea (or a dram) for the women. And silver coins would be slipped under the baby's pillow. This still happens today, though silver sixpences have mostly disappeared!

Font stones, stones roughly hollowed to form a shallow basin are found in, or near, old churches. Later, more elaborate ones, often of marble, were made. In the wood, on Loch Ness side, near Abriachan, is a large stone with a hollow in which there is always, inexplicably, water. It is known as St Columba's Font Stone. The Saint was in the area and he was known to have a special concern for women in childbirth. Almost within living memory women would come at night to take a bottle of water from the font to help a neighbour giving birth and to give the baby a surreptitious extra baptism.

Babies who died unbaptised could not be buried in the church graveyard. They were laid to rest, between sundown and sunrise, in some remote spot, often among rocks, which does seem a hard-hearted practice. A dead baby's things were all burned.

As soon as she had recovered her strength the mother would be 'churched'. This meant walking three times round the church, sunwise, before attending the service. After that, she had peace to enjoy this new member of the family. But still the fairies must be placated. No-one must praise the child's beauty, for this would encourage those predators. Even in our own day this attitude is present. Praise of beauty or skills in a child is not happily accepted.

For those early women the customs associated with childbirth, with the sense of community that they evoked, must surely have been helpful at this traumatic time. The clinical atmosphere of hospital birthing does seem unfeeling by comparison. Many women these days are opting for home birth, though the 'nine little wavelets of grace' may be forgotten.

CHAPTER 8

Witchcraft

A DASTARDLY FORM of persecution to which women were submitted from very early times was that of being accused of witchcraft.

In 1597 King James VI published his book *Daemonologie*. He had an obsession with witchcraft, believing that witches had raised the storm which threatened him on his voyage from Denmark to fetch his wife. John Knox, the great Protestant reformer, preached against 'the Devil, the Mass and Witches'. These women were accused of being in league with the devil, capable not only of raising storms, but of harming cattle and other beasts, those mainstays of the people, of souring milk and of actually causing the death of a disliked person by making a clay image of him or her and sticking pins into it.

In the western Highlands and in the Islands, where people's lives were intensely linked to natural phenomena which were sometimes strange enough, witches were mostly tolerated as part of the order of things. There was not the merciless hunting of them found elsewhere in the country and, indeed, in other parts of the world. Here, witches did not ride on broomsticks, though they could transform themselves into creatures such as the hare.

Belief in the power of the 'evil eye', that a man or woman could cast a spell to damage another, was widespread. Alexander Carmichael, in his wonderful collection of charms, prayers, incantations and blessings gathered from the people of the islands, quotes a charm to counteract the spell cast by the 'evil eye':

Charm for evil eye
I make for thee
Charms for evil eye
In reliance on Peter and on Paul
And on quiet Brigid, my beloved.

It continues for many verses. The healing skills which some women, known as 'white witches', possessed were very real and effective. If a little bit of trickery went with them, such as adding silver to the water used, or tying a red thread to the cow's tail, that dash of magic was all to the good. Belief in the healing was what mattered. It was probably just an advanced form of the natural healing processes, using plants, which had been long known. But the very efficacy of the treatment which these skilled women could give was therefore deemed magical and those who practised it were considered 'unchancy beings' and so were called witches.

Katherine Ross, Lady Foulis

In the eastern Highlands many instances of witchcraft have been recorded. On 22 June 1590, Katherine Ross, Lady Foulis, and her stepson Hector Munro were tried in Edinburgh for 'witchcraft incantation, sorcery and poisoning'. It is a long and complicated story. For personal reasons Lady Foulis wished to see her older stepson, Robert, dead. Also, so that Robert's widow could then marry her brother, George Ross of Balnagowan, his wife, Lady Balnagowan, had to be disposed of. To realise these 'death wishes' Lady Foulis consulted many witches. Clay images of the intended victims were made and shot with 'elf-arrows' – Stone Age flint arrow heads. Poisons were concocted.

Hector was accused of taking part in various 'devilish' practices.

Some of them were probably indulged in as a form of macabre entertainment, but nevertheless he had to stand trial. Both he and Lady Foulis were acquitted, their defence being largely in the hands of the nobility. Meanwhile, various minions who had assisted in the nefarious ploys were put to death.

The Millburn valley, near Inverness, was a centre of witchcraft. Many old women lived there, in small dwellings. One, 'Creibh Mhor', and her sister, in 1603, made a clay effigy of Cuthbert of Castlehill, a big man in the district. Pins were stuck in the figure. It was found and the two women were burnt to death.

In Auldearn, some miles east of Inverness, in 1662, Isobel Gowdie was convicted of witchcraft. After torture, lack of food, being beaten, kept without sleep and having her limbs crushed in a vice, she confessed to having met the devil and consecrated herself to his service. She made three confessions, some to elders of the kirk, seeming to revel in relating the enormity of her sins. The outcome of the trial has not been recorded, but doubtless she perished.

In that same year, the Chisholm of Strathglass, wanting to be rid of a body of MacLeans who had become 'kindly tenants', that is, tenants claiming kinship, on his land, arranged for them to be accused of witchcraft. At that time the practice was being condemned in an hysterical style. A body of men had set themselves up in a professional guild, demanding high fees for their services as 'witch prickers'. The services consisted in pricking the body of a supposed witch with a long steel needle in an attempt to find a spot insensitive to pain, known as the 'devil's mark'. In this way many innocent women were convicted and put to death.

Eventually several 'prickers' were imprisoned when it was discovered they were acting solely out of greed or malice. One 'pricker', at Wardlaw, near Kirkhill, was found to be a woman disguised as a man. Most of her victims were released. The

MacLeans who had been accused of witchcraft appealed to their chief and the accusations were annulled.

The last judicial execution for witchcraft took place in Dornoch in 1727. Janet Horne was accused of 'having ridden upon her own daughter transformed into a pony and shod by the devil'. It was as a result of this, the court declared, that the girl was lame in both feet and had paralysed hands. Her mother was condemned and burnt to death in a tar barrel. An inscribed stone marks the spot.

Not long after this occurrence, in 1736, an Act was passed making the maximum penalty for 'pretended' witchcraft one year's imprisonment. The Age of Enlightenment had dawned!

Today, many of the healing practices of the so-called 'white' witches are being studied and their worth appreciated. The psychological element is much in tune with modern thinking. Furthermore, people living isolated lives, by choice or as a result of circumstances, are no longer looked on askance. If they prefer to abide by older customs and beliefs they are treated with tolerance and respect.

CHAPTER 9

Women of the '45 – the Rebel Women

FLORA MACDONALD MAY have inherited all the glory of having helped Prince Charles to escape his captors after his defeat at the battle of Culloden in 1746, but many other women had put themselves at risk on his behalf from the day of his arrival a year earlier. Their belief in the validity of the Jacobite cause, on which they had been nurtured from an early age, was so strong, that it outweighed all fear of any consequences of their support of the Young Pretender.

Charles was young, he was handsome, he was full of confidence and hope. To rally to his standard was a privilege. This was how the Jacobite women saw things.

Jenny Cameron of Glendessary

Jenny Cameron raised 300 men and led them to Glenfinnan where the Prince had landed. Was this unwomanly behaviour? It seems the Hanoverian propagandists considered it so. Jenny Cameron was accused of sexual misconduct of many kinds, including seducing the prince. In fact she was a robust young woman who lived out a life of Jacobite activities, was taken into custody by the Hanoverians and eventually retreated into anonymity and founded a school for orphans of the uprising. At the site of her grave in East Kilbride, whither she had fled to escape persecution in the Highlands, her life is faithfully recorded on a plaque.

Isabel Haldane of Ardsheal

Isabel taunted her husband Charles Stewart, saying 'you stay at home, I will command the Appin men'. Goaded thus he raised a company of some 300 to join the prince as he moved on, becoming a member of his council of war. Later, after hiding in caves, he escaped, as so many did after the failure of the uprising, to France, while his pregnant wife remained at Ardsheal. Here, Hanoverian troops attacked, and ransacked the house, forcing Isabel, in swirling snow, to give birth to a daughter in an outhouse. Eventually she managed to join her husband in France.

Lady Margaret Ogilvy

At just twenty years old, Lady Ogilvy travelled with her husband on the campaign into England, despite the fact that women were not supposed to accompany the men. After the battle of Culloden she was arrested and imprisoned, eventually escaping, disguised as a man, to France, where she joined her husband. Their reunion was short-lived for her health deteriorated and she died young.

Colonel Anne

Lady MacKintosh, née Anne Farquharson of Invercauld, was an ardent Jacobite. While her husband, a Hanoverian supporter, was away with the Black Watch regiment, she rode round the country-side, wearing a tartan habit and a blue bonnet, carrying a bag of money and two pistols. An attractive, vivacious young woman, she was known as 'Colonel Anne' as she lured men into joining the rebel forces. She sheltered Prince Charles and a body of his followers at her home, Moy Hall, allowing them time to escape when danger was near. 'La belle rebelle' the prince called her. Then a party of officers and 200 men was sent out from Inverness to arrest her at Moy, to arrest the woman they called 'that bloody rebel.' After looting the house they forced her to ride to Inverness where she was imprisoned for several weeks. Eventually she met the Duke of Cumberland, and was then released into her husband's custody. She and Angus, whom she loved dearly, in spite of their differing political allegiances, lived happily together for a good many years.

The savagery of the aftermath of the battle of Culloden has been recorded by Bishop Forbes in his book *The Lyon in Mourning*. Women were raped as a form of subjection, yet many of them carried on fearlessly, helping in any way possible the Jacobite cause. As soon as the fighting was over, some went onto the battlefield, carrying bandages and blankets, tending to the wounded. Many offered food and lodging and comfort to the able. They visited the prisons, begging for better conditions for the men. In their homes they made white cockades, symbols of loyalty to King James.

The wealthy gave money to the cause. These women were attacked ferociously in pamphlets issued by the government. Some were arrested and transported to London by sea in atrocious ship-board conditions. Many were imprisoned on false charges. To drink a Jacobite toast was treason.

Some were sent overseas as 'indentured servants', that is to say slaves. Class distinctions prevailed. The clan chiefs' wives – Lady MacKinnon and Lady Clanranald, in particular – were held in private houses in London. These were the houses of 'messengers', that is, servants of the government. In one house, that of Mr and Mrs Money, conditions were somewhat better than those of the prisons, but very cramped. The women longed for fresh air. Lady

Clanranald suffered from severe depression. After the amnesty most were released in 1747.

Many tales were told, of course, of romantic attachments to the Prince. It is unlikely, however, that his thoughts would have been on anything but survival in the days of wandering after Culloden. He was dishevelled, perpetually tired, hungry and thirsty, often suffering from dysentery. One exception was his liaison with Clementine Walkinshaw, whom he met in Glasgow after the retreat from Derby in early 1746. She was a bright and caring person and she had a daughter to the Prince named Charlotte. Clementine lived with the Prince, on and off for many years. Charlotte looked after her father in his sad old age.

Lady Nairne, a member of a staunchly Jacobite family, and a considerable poet, wrote many attractive songs in the late 18th century, including 'Charlie is my darling' and 'Wha'll be King but Charlie.' Hopes of a resurgence of Jacobitism died hard.

The women of the clansmen's families did not see things in quite that light. Many had been widowed, many had lost their homes, some their children. Others had been raped, tortured, imprisoned, transported into slavery. Many of those who survived were left in a state of near starvation as their stock was looted and their crops trampled by the marauding soldiers. The attempts to eradicate the 'barbarians' of the Highlands were ghastly.

Meanwhile, in Edinburgh, the ladies in tartan finery could dance away the days and nights pledging secret toasts to the Young Pretender, now 'over the water', to the tune of 'Will you no come back again?'

One woman involved with the Prince during the post-Culloden period, though not exactly a rebel, whose life has been fully recorded was Flora MacDonald.

CHAPTER 10

Flora MacDonald (1722–1790) – A Reluctant Heroine

AT MILTON, IN THE island of South Uist, stands a small cairn with this inscription, undated:

> Clan Donald raised this cairn of remembrance to their kinswoman Flora MacDonald, daughter of Ranald, son of Angus of Milton, South Uist. She was born in 1722 near this place and spent her early life in the place that stood on this foundation. When pursuit was drawing near to the Prince in the Long Island she greatly aided him by her heroism and endurance to gain shelter in the Isle of Skye.

Nothing but a few scattered stones remains of the house where Flora was born. The site is not sign-posted. And she does not figure in the oral tradition of the Islands. The Prince himself is not in the league of heroes, though his courage and endurance were admired. As we have seen, his coming brought so much trouble to so many.

Flora herself was to be very much a part of her times, involved in the aftermath of Culloden, the saga of the Prince and later, the American War of Independence. Her father died a year after she was born, leaving her mother with a family to bring up and two farms to run. After four years of struggle as a widow she married 'one-eyed' Hugh MacDonald of Sleat, in Skye, a kinsman of hers. This was a happy marriage. Thereafter Flora divided her time between South Uist and Skye.

The Chief's wife, known as Lady Clan, wife of Clanranald,

had helped the family during their difficult times after the death of Flora's father. She became a friend to Flora as she grew up, having her in the house at Nunton where she picked up the social graces of singing, dancing and playing the spinet, an early form of harpsichord or piano. She also learnt to speak English.

By the time of the Rising of 1745 Flora was an attractive and accomplished young woman of 23. In June of the following year, when the Prince was being harried, she found herself in her old home ground on South Uist, not far from his hiding place. To her surprise one day, her brother Angus asked her to go up to a shieling, in a remote place in the hills, on her own in the evening. There she was sleeping when her cousin Neil MacEachan arrived to waken her. She had scarcely dressed when the Prince was at the door. He greeted her with courtesy. All she had to offer him, as hospitality demanded, was a bowl of cream. He took it hungrily. Captain Felix O'Neil, who was with the Prince, then explained to Flora the plan they had devised to get Charles to Skye. He was to be disguised as her servant girl!

At first Flora refused to accept the idea, fearing for the reflection on her chief and also on herself. The Prince pleaded with her. He was clearly depressed and exhausted and suffering from scurvy. It was a point of honour, of course, to help anyone in need. Reluctantly, she agreed to the plan.

The decision taken, at daybreak Flora set off to the Clanranald house at Nunton where she and Lady Clan got busy preparing for the journey and making clothes the Prince could wear in his disguise as Betty Burke. He wanted to carry a pistol under his skirts, but only a cudgel was allowed.

At last, after much changing of plans and much dodging of militiamen, with the prince getting ever more anxious, they set sail in a small boat from Benbecula; the Prince, Flora, Neil MacEachain and five crew. The crossing through the summer night was stormy, but the Prince was in a cheerful mood, singing Jacobite songs and protecting Flora as she slept. The landing was not easy, as government troops and warships were about, but eventually Charles was taken to a place of safety. Then it was possible to escape to Portree, where he said farewell to Flora. His travails were not over but he would get further help from the MacKinnons of Skye and others to see him to the mainland and his eventual rescue.

Flora had helped him to overcome his immediate troubles, but her own were just beginning. Rumours of her involvement with the Prince were going from hushed mouth to hushed mouth; betrayal was rife, fear of prosecution was very real. On 12 July, on her way to Armadale, she was arrested and taken aboard the *Furnace*, the ship commanded by the notorious Captain Ferguson. Conditions on board were appalling; prisoners kept below decks, sleeping on bare boards, little food provided. Men were tortured, beaten with the cat o'nine tails. Flora stood up to questioning and was treated with respect. She was even allowed ashore, under guard, to say goodbye to her mother.

She was later transferred to another naval vessel, the *Bridgewater*, with a captain who treated her well. Arriving at Leith in early September she was allowed visitors aboard. She met Robert Forbes, the Episcopal clergyman who was collecting stories of the atrocities committed by the Hanoverian troops. She was reluctant to disclose much of her experiences.

On arrival in London she was briefly imprisoned. Then, after pleas for special treatment, she was sent to the house of William Dick, a 'messenger' who took in prisoners.

It was still a time of fear and anxiety for known or suspected Jacobites, a time of killings, shootings, hangings. In April of the following year Lord Lovat was beheaded, to the acclaim of a blood-thirsty mob. Curiously enough, Flora was received by Frederick, Prince of Wales, brother of the infamous Duke of Cumberland. He procured comforts for her. This may have been because he actually hated his brother. Lady Primrose, a Jacobite aristocrat, raised a fortune on Flora's behalf from among wealthy London Jacobites. Soon the amnesty of 1747 meant that she could be released.

On her return to Skye she was not as warmly welcomed as she had anticipated. Were her folk wondering where her true loyalty lay?

The following year she returned to London, where she was fussed over by the Jacobites and had her portrait painted by Allan Ramsay. Back in Skye, she received a proposal of marriage from Allan MacDonald, factor to the MacDonald of Sleat, a handsome, well set-up young man, one of the 'kin'. In 1750 they were married at Armadale.

Allan had progressive ideas in farming – crop rotation and the out-wintering of cattle. Some of his 'improvements' were costly and involved the estate in debt. Soon, Flora's fortune was swallowed up. Allan's financial disasters led to his dismissal from his post as factor, though he and the family stayed on at Kingsborough. Here, in 1773, they were visited by Johnson and Boswell on their tour through the islands. The doctor was much taken with Flora. Boswell described her as 'a little woman of genteel appearance and uncommonly mild and well bred'.

Over the years she and Allan had seven children, five boys and two girls. However, things were not going well on Skye, overall. Bad harvests had caused conditions of near-starvation. Chiefs were demanding increases in rents. Emigration was clearly on the horizon.

Flora's step-father Hugh had gone to North Carolina in 1773.

The following year, Flora and Allan with two of their sons, Alexander and James, arrived there. They settled at Cheek's Creek, where there was a small, scattered community of Highland people. Here they acquired 70 acres of reasonably good ground, with apple and peach orchards.

The forest was always there, ready to take over again, and the wild animals were not far away. They had eight servants, three women and five men as well as their two sons to do the work of cultivation. Flora had brought furniture, silver and books from home so it looked as though life could go forward happily. But among the longer-established settlers there were murmurs of discontent with the way they were being treated by the governor of the Province. Allan MacDonald, who often wore Highland dress and liked to see himself as a Chieftain in his new domain, had sworn loyalty to the Crown as an officer in the army. So it was that he was easily persuaded to come out on the Loyalist side in the coming conflict with the rebellious settlers. A body of men called the Royal Highland Emigrants was formed and while Allan and his sons were away soldiering Flora was left to cope with harvests in the torrid summer heat.

Things came to a head in 1776 when the Loyalist Army was defeated at the famous battle of Moore's Creek, another Culloden, when broadswords and desperate bravery went under to musket-fire and trickery. Allan and his sons were taken prisoner.

For Flora this was a time of great distress. Even her servants turned against her. Plunderers were everywhere. As a result of the misery she contracted a fever. When James was able to escape and get home to tell her that his father and brother were safe she recovered her strength and was able to ride out visiting the loyal colonists to bring them some comfort. On one of these rides she fell from her horse and broke her arm. The pain resulting from this accident was to last all her life. For two years she suffered insults and robbery, losing the precious silver she had brought from home.

When Allan was eventually allowed parole he went to New York to arrange an exchange of prisoners. Flora managed to join him there, before travelling on with him to Nova Scotia. Lonely and miserable in this bleak place she grew homesick for Skye and her own kin. Allan arranged for her to sail home before another winter set in.

Reaching London towards the end of 1779 Flora again succumbed to illness, brought on by the turbulence of the passage during which she injured her other arm. Some Jacobites in the city looked after her for several months until she was able the following spring to travel on to Edinburgh, then to Dunvegan on Skye where her married daughter lived. From there, with no settled home of her own, she moved to South Uist to stay with her son at Milton, then back to Skye, to her daughter.

When the war in America ended in 1782, Alan was retired on half pay, received a land grant in Nova Scotia and some compensation for the losses endured during the campaign. He cleared a few acres on this holding and built a small house where he hoped he and Flora could live out their lives. But the half pay and meagre compensation were not enough for this dream to be fulfilled.

In 1785 Allan returned to Skye, where he was able to take over the lease of a small place near their old home at Kingsborough. Both now old and frail – Flora suffering from arthritis in both her arms and Allan having lost the use of his legs after the long spell of imprisonment – they had the happiness of being together, with four of their children not far away. Their son Johnnie, who had done very well in India, now settled an annuity on his mother, not his father, whose mismanagement of money he remembered.

This happy life was only to last for five years. Flora died aged 68 and was buried at Kilmore on the north coast of Skye. Several thousand people from many parts of the Highlands attended her funeral. Like a true Highlander she had played down her part in any heroics. For this she was respected. Allan died two and a half years later.

In 1801 Johnnie returned from India and had a memorial stone erected over his parents' grave. On it he had inscribed Dr Johnson's words regarding Flora: 'a name that will be mentioned in history and, if courage and fidelity be virtues, mentioned with honour'. Sadly, this memorial was desecrated by people removing pieces of marble as mementoes of the famous woman. Seventy years later an Iona cross was put up in her memory, but this was blown down in a storm. Finally, a second cross was erected, with a strong iron support. In 1899 a statue was built in Inverness, showing Flora, her dog at her feet, looking towards the west.

In Nova Scotia Flora is remembered, as is Allan. Several educational establishments bear her name. North Carolina remains the most strongly Highland Scottish of all the States. Since 1956 Highland Games, based on those held at Braemar in Scotland, called Grandfather Mountain Games, have been held every year over a weekend in July.

After her death, unlikely legends of all kinds grew around Flora's name, including that of a love affair with Prince Charles. Highly inaccurate biographies were written, also poems and songs. These are forgotten. What remains in the minds of most of her kin is her steadfastness in the fighting of lost causes, her care for her family and her upholding of traditional values.

Anne Grant of Laggan (1755–1838) 'She was a lady most complete and bright.'[1]

ANOTHER WOMAN OF THE Highlands who had experience of the war in America was Anne Grant of Laggan (1755–1838). Anne Grant was a remarkable woman. Her *Letters from the Mountains* are perhaps the best-known of her writings, but there is much more to her work. Almost entirely untutored during her early years, she ended her long life with a circle of literary friends and admirers which included Sir Walter Scott, Henry MacKenzie and many others. Her gifts of perception, of imaginative under-standing of people and places, found expression in all that she wrote – poetry, essays, letters. She was born in Glasgow in 1755 of Highland parentage, her father, Duncan MacVicar, being a member of an Argyllshire family, her mother a Stewart of Appin. At barely three years old she was taken by her mother to America, to join her father, who had given up his business and was serving in Montgomerie's regiment, the 77th Foot. They settled in Albany, 200 miles up the Hudson river, where the regiment was stationed near a group of Dutch immigrants.

It was a lonely life for a child, with no schooling, without the companionship of other children. 'I had no companion... did not until the 6th year of my age possess a single toy', she was to write

---

[1] The description of William Wallace's mother from *Blind Harry's Wallace*

later. Her mother taught her to read and write, to sew and to knit. In a book written in much later life, after the publication of the *Letters*, a book she called *Memoirs of an American Lady, with Sketches of Manners and Scenery in America as they existed previous to the Revolution*, she gives a moving and evocative picture of her young years and of the way of life in the America of her time.

Anne and her mother would accompany her father on his travels round the country on army business. Sometimes the journeys were perilous enough, by raft on turbulent rivers, but Anne revelled in the life, acquiring first-hand knowledge of animals, birds, trees, plants, the whole set-up of the natural world. Her mind was being stretched in other ways. A kindly Scottish sergeant would read *Blind Harry's Wallace* to her. This gave her a passionate longing to know Scotland.

One day, with her parents visiting a Captain Mungo Campbell, she 'was much captivated with the copper-plates in an edition of *Paradise Lost* which, on that account, he had given me to admire. When I was going away he said to me 'Keep that book, my dear child. I foretell that the time will come when you will take pleasure in it'.' Overjoyed at receiving the book, but vexed that she could not understand much of it, she had recourse to a tattered dictionary and puzzled out every word, learning many lines by heart. After that, at eight years old, she read everything she could lay hands on.

At about this time she became the protégée of Madame Schuyler, the grande dame of the Dutch colony, who encouraged her in intellectual pursuits. She spent much time in the Dutch family's big house, listening to the adults, reading, talking, joining in discussion. The Dutch had some slaves, as was the custom, but, she says, did not ill-treat them. They were 'young negroes whom it was the custom to rear very tenderly, and instruct very carefully.'

Soon Anne came to know, respect and admire the Mohawk

Indians in whose lands the colonists lived. These Mohawks were helpful and often offered protection to the Europeans against unfriendly tribes. She refutes the accusation of idleness made against them, saying 'the indolence with which we reproach them is merely the consequence of their commercial intercourse with us and the fatal passion for strong liquors which resulted from it.' Many Indians died of diseases brought in by Europeans, in particular, smallpox. She believed that 'northern nations were instructed in the Arts of Life by those they had subdued'. 'Why should any man desire to possess more than he uses?' an Indian asks. One Englishman in the colony who had a 'hypochondriac disorder' went to live with some Indians, adopting their dress and manners. He stayed for two years and was cured. As she learnt a little of their language, Anne was increasingly able to appreciate the good breeding of the Indians, observing their courtesy when, for instance, they would never interrupt a speaker. She also came to understand that, to them, revenge was a virtue, retaliation a duty. Unprovoked, they preferred the pipe of peace and took great pleasure in the wearing of elaborate dress and the carrying of ornamented weapons. Many converted to Christianity. The voices of the women, Anne says, were particularly sweet and powerful. The young Indians played football and shinty with the soldiers. In her future relations with the Highland people among whom she was to live she must often have thought back to her contacts with these other native people whom she admired and loved.

As discontent with their treatment by the home country – the Stamp Act, the imposition of import duties – grew among the British settlers, many foresaw the imminence of a breakdown in the relationship. Anne records in particular the forebodings of Madame Schuyler. She also records the arrival of William Penn, with his high ideals and says of the Quakers that they were 'the only Europeans in the new world who always treated the Indians with probity like their own and with kindness calculated to do honour to the faith they professed.' Regarding slaves, she says they 'voluntarily gave freedom to those whom they held in easy bondage.'

When the time came for his regiment to return home, Anne's father acquired a considerable amount of land, partly granted, partly bought from others, on which he proposed to settle. She herself, still very much the protégée of Madame Schuyler, was looked upon as an heiress, with a young negro servant, Marion, and a pony to ride. But trouble was brewing. The land was intruded upon and eventually confiscated by Republican interests, as MacVicar was looked on as a Royalist. So, in 1768 the family returned to Scotland and he resumed his business in Glasgow.

In these two volumes of *Memoirs* we find a story of the life and times of early settlers in America and of their contacts with the native peoples which must be a valuable source for historians of the period. Written by one who, in her early and impressionable years, was involved in the events and situations described, they have all the freshness of actuality.

After returning home, Anne was to spend a few years living a pleasant enough life in the Glasgow area, where she met young women who were to become lifelong friends and the recipients of her future letters. There was still no question of further education for her. Then in 1773, her father, anxious to return to army life, became Barrack Master at Fort Augustus. There, Anne fell in love with the Highland country. She walked, she rode, she sailed in the Governor's galley on Loch Ness. She visited the Grants of Invermoriston, the Frasers of Foyers, and made many friends in Inverness. Still an avid reader, she relished the recently published poems of Ossian and began to write verse.

Soon she was to meet the Rev. James Grant of Strathspey,

who was chaplain to the garrison. Finding a compatibility of mind and spirit, they became well acquainted and in 1779 they married. Her young husband had been appointed to the charge of parish minister in Laggan. They made their way there by coach, by the direct route, General Wade's road over the Corryarrick pass. On arrival, they found themselves housed in a small cottage at the farm of Gaskbeg. There was no church in the parish, only preaching sites, no manse, no glebe. They were to receive an extra £20 a year to compensate for the lack of a manse. Being of a happy disposition they soon settled into the life, enjoying, when time allowed, companionable walks in the meadows and along the riverside.

It was a busy life. Five children were born in the early years of the marriage, another seven were to follow. Sadly, three of the youngest died of measles during a severe epidemic. From the letters Anne wrote to her friends at this time (later to be published as *Letters from the Mountains*), there emerges a picture of the places and the people among whom she lived. Determined not to be a 'stranger' in her husband's country, she visited the people in their homes, attending evening ceilidhs and setting herself to learn the Gaelic language. She says:

> I was assiduous in learning the language of the country where my lot was thrown. Long days have I knit my stocking or carried an infant from sheaf to sheaf, sitting and walking by turns on the harvest field, attentively observing conversation... I was captivated with the strength and beauty of their expression in their native tongue.

Shortly afterwards she says of her children, 'I never desire to hear an English word out of their mouths till they are four or five years old.' She had her own ideas on education, declaring: '[I shall] make an experiment on my mountain nymphs. I propose, in the first place, to attend, above all things, to the culture of the heart... in due time to the understanding.' She was thus in advance of some similar contemporary thinking on the subject.

When her father removed to Fort George some of the children were sent there, to be cared for by her mother. 'We went to Fort George in the little machine,' she says. This was a gig. At the Fort she enjoyed, during a short visit, the elegant life of the officers and their families. Later, her father, retired on half-pay, was to go back to Glasgow and there to attend to the formal education of the older children.

Meanwhile, Anne was busy with the duties of a minister's wife and also with farming activities. The Duke of Gordon had kindly allowed them to lease the farm of Gaskbeg, where they had a considerable acreage of land, cows, sheep, horses, pigs and poultry, and grew oats, barley, flax and potatoes. They were thus self-sufficient in food (only luxuries such as tea and sugar coming from Inverness) and made their own garments and footwear. In her letters Anne describes life on the farm, her joy in the seasons and in particular the summer days at the shielings, when the cattle, some sheep and the horses were taken up to the high pastures. Anne also made a garden, planted apple trees, grew soft fruit and many vegetables. She had knowledge of healing from the plant lore of the Indians and was able to apply this in times of sickness. Her love of the people and her respect for them grew as she came to know them well.

This was a time of great disturbance in the lives of all Highland people. Many of them still remembered the horrors of the aftermath of the Battle of Culloden: the killing, the burning and raping. They deplored the presence of the 'Red Soldiers', as the occupying forces were known. The 'improvements' in agricultural practice had already led to the expulsion of some tenants from their holdings, and more were being 'cleared' from the land to make way for large flocks of sheep. A pithy observer of the Highland Clearances, Anne wrote in one of her letters in 1791: 'The only cause of complaint in Scotland is the rage for sheep-farming'. Her love and admiration for the people increased. 'There is a musician in every house and a poet in every hamlet', she writes. When the people were being encouraged to abandon their holdings to settle in planned villages and engage in crafts, Anne remarked 'a Highlander never sits easy at a loom; 'tis like putting a deer in the plough.'

By 1786 a church had been built for the Laggan parish. Later there was to be a manse. But the family continued to live at Gaskbeg, a place they had come to love. Then, in 1801, Anne's husband, a delicate man, died quite suddenly after an illness of three days. Her grief is vividly expressed in her letters. For two years she stayed on at the farm, then, with eight children and a burden of debt, she went to live near Stirling.

Here she had a garden and some ground where she could 'keep two cows'. With a small pension from her husband's chaplaincy duties she could manage to live simply, but there was nothing to spare. When a daughter living in England fell ill, probably with tuberculosis, money had to be found for a cure. There was much sympathy for her. She and her husband had been well liked in the parish. Friends persuaded her to publish her poems in the hope of some financial reward. A list of 3,000 subscribers to the resultant book included Sir Walter Scott, Henry MacKenzie and other well-known people. The volume, which was published in 1803, was entitled *The Highlanders and other Poems* and was dedicated 'To her Grace the Duchess of Gordon these

poems are respectfully inscribed by her Grace's humble servant the
Author, Anne Grant.' This was the usual somewhat obsequious
style of the time.

In the book is a poem to Sir James Grant, the 'Good Sir
James' as he was known, who had done his best for the tenants
on his land, and a song written for the departure of the Marquis
of Huntly, the Duke of Gordon's son, with his regiment in 1799
– 'Oh where, tell me where, is your Highland laddie gone?'
which, to the air of 'The Bluebells of Scotland' is still sung today.

The notes on the poems give a picture of life in the Highlands
at the time, glimpses of historical events and Anne's ideas on emigration. The loss of so many valued people was something she
deplored. Also included in the volume are some translations from
the Gaelic. The book was widely acclaimed and a second edition
was eventually published.

Several poems, or 'songs', of hers were included in a book
brought out at this time by George Thomson, Burns' publisher. In
this are many poems (set to music and so called 'songs'), by Burns,
as well as many of traditional origin. Thomson says, in a footnote:

After this volume was printed off the Editor received a
letter from Mrs Grant earnestly requesting him that her
name might not be prefixed to her songs. Had this request
reached him in time he certainly must have complied with it;
although he conceives there are few authors who would
not be proud to own such beautiful productions.

Meanwhile her son Duncan, who had received a commission in
the military service of the East India Company, needed money
for his equipment. Anne, whose reputation as a writer was now
established, was persuaded by friends to embark on the publication

of her letters. At first reluctant to do so for reasons of discretion, she eventually agreed and was pleasantly surprised when a Mr Longman (described as a Bookseller, but who must have been the ancestor of the well-known publisher of today) in London, willingly accepted the task of printing the letters. In the summer of 1806 the book, *Letters from the Mountains*, appeared and was an instant success. Several editions were later to be published. Some good ladies in Boston, America, made a reprint at their own expense, for which Anne received a welcome sum. She was a prolific letter-writer, composing almost every other day, 'early morning in summer, late evening in winter' as she describes it. As well as the pictures of her own life and surroundings which she paints in such an evocative style, there are glimpses of other parts of the Highlands, as in this description of Knoydart, as it was then. She calls it:

> A wondrous region. There the natives are looked upon happier than others. There is abundant grass and luxuriant heath. Deer, wild fowl and fish are in great plenty. All this they enjoy without a rival or competitor, for who could go for it or carry it away? A bishop... spends his life in this truly savage abode.

The greatest value of her chronicles of life in the Highlands of her time is that they are, as she says herself 'a pastoral written by a real shepherd'. She writes as one who lived and worked among the people, sharing their experiences, not, as was happening at the time, as a traveller or an inquisitor, reporting superficial impressions. She saw the whole lives of the people, as she had seen the Indians and the European settlers during her years in America.

The success of the *Letters* must have pleased her and the

pecuniary reward must have been welcome, but Anne's personal life was dogged by sorrow. In 1807 two of her daughters, Charlotte and Catherine, died, probably of tuberculosis. By this time the family was scattered to various parts of the country. She herself was spending time in the homes of a growing number of friends, and continuing to write prolifically. James MacPherson, her friend and neighbour, who also maintained a voluminous correspondence, would sometimes help by 'franking' her letters along with his, to save the quite considerable cost of postage. Reviews of the *Letters* in various literary journals were mixed, but Anne was not deterred by even the most damning. She was well aware of her own deficiencies of style, but was determined to keep to her own way. And the book continued to sell.

In the early part of the following year she set out, at the insistence of several friends, to write what was originally to be the biography of her oldest friend, Aunt Schuyler of Albany, but which turned into *Memoirs of an American Lady*, published in 1808. In its pages we can see Anne as a child, growing 'tall and awkward' as she says herself, abandoning her dancing lessons, but revelling in her natural surroundings, reading widely and becoming the much-loved protégée of her adopted 'Aunt'. The *Memoirs* went to the press that autumn, dedicated to Sir William Grant, the Master of the Rolls, who, in Anne's words, 'seems much disposed to take an interest in what concerns me.' By the following year a new edition appeared. Some alterations to the text had been suggested – 'to obliterate certain familiar and colloquial sets of phrase', but they came too late, for which the author was thankful, as she wished 'on all occasions, in public and private, to be my very self.'

She was now living in Edinburgh and undertaking the education of her friends' children along with that of the younger members of her own family. She took an active part in the literary life of the city, meeting Sir Walter Scott, Francis Jeffrey, editor of the famous *Edinburgh Review*, Henry MacKenzie and many others, attending dinner parties and reading all the new books. It was an exciting time for the writers, artists, critics, lawyers, medical men, philosophers, preachers, publishers and printers, all working in the still bright aura of the 'Enlightenment'. The friendships, feuds, jealousies, and hopes of a vibrant society are all there in full measure.

By 1811 Anne was busy writing again and in that year her book *Essays on the Superstitions of the Highlands* was published. In these essays she shows her innate understanding of the Highland psyche with its 'visionary modes of thinking'. The courteous manners and ways of speech common to the Highlands stem, she says, from the frequent intercourse of the people among themselves, at daily work, at evening ceilidhs, with their 'open-hearted gaiety and stingless raillery', when the oral tradition of reciting tales and poems kept their minds alive. Their regard for their progenitors was strong – 'no Highlander thought of himself as an individual'. In former times, when the land was shared under the 'runrig' system and the people were not restricted in small, enclosed plots, or 'crofts', there was 'much debate and consultation' among them. The Highland peasant has been, for ages, 'the most accommodating, most reflecting and deliberating.'

Anne's history reports clearly what was happening at the start of the Agricultural Revolution, when developments of all kinds were taking place – new roads allowing better communication with the south, schools with English as the teaching medium being established, the people being persuaded to adapt to resettlement in villages, if they did not emigrate. Anne commented:

> Every attempt at sudden improvement so entirely damages
> it [the system of life in the Highlands] and a sort of
> inverted benevolence seems to invade every plan for the
> improvement of the Highlands... except that of teaching
> the natives to read the scriptures in their own language.

Francis Jeffery, editor of the *Edinburgh Review*, issued, as was his
wont, a scathing criticism of the essays, saying they were charac-
terised by 'an active, ambitious and somewhat ill-regarded fantasy'.
Though his remarks must have been hurtful, Anne realised that
the Edinburgh literati, with the exception of Sir Walter Scott,
knew and cared little about the Highland people, regarding them
as rebellious and unlettered. She went on, quite undaunted, to
publish three years later a poem entitled simply '1813', in which
she praises the Celtic race, this for the edification, she hopes, of
that galaxy of intellectuals living in Edinburgh.

There was still much anxiety and sadness in her life. Her
daughter Anne and her son Duncan, in India, both died at this time.
She was to publish no more work, but she was still very much part
of the literary and social life of the city, her visitors list including
Robert Southey, Thomas Campbell, Thomas Chalmers, de Quincey,
Christopher North, Henry Raeburn and of course, Sir Walter, of
whom she was fond, describing him thus: 'his simplicity of manners,
his ever good humour and that same sense and genuine truth – that
most unostentatious yet ever-waking benevolence'.

In 1820, after a fall near her house in Princes Street, Anne was
incapacitated for quite a time. A lack of her usual mobility caused
her to become over-heavy. She still managed, nevertheless, to travel
about and to visit many friends.

After the harsh criticism of her work by Francis Jeffery, who
was also a fierce critic of Byron and of many others, Anne must

have been gratified, in 1821, to receive from the Highland Society of London the Gold Medal for the best Essay on the 'Past and Present State of the Highlands'.

However, Anne was still to know more sorrow. In that same year her daughter with the strange name of Moore died, aged 25. Two years later she lost Isabella, then Mary, her last remaining daughter. She was left with John Peter, her son and the only child who was to survive her. He came to live with her, looking after her devotedly and working as a lawyer from their shared house, Brae House, near St Cuthbert's church. It was a house she came to love, with a garden and huge trees.

By this time she had been granted a small pension by the king on the representation of Sir Walter Scott and other friends, for 'the services she has rendered to the cause of religion, morality, knowledge and taste'. This, together with an annuity from Sir William Grant, who, she said, had been 'more than a brother to me', a few bequests and the proceeds of her writing, allowed her to live in simple comfort and to receive her many friends. She especially welcomed those who came from America and brought her news of that remembered country of her early youth. Though often confined to a wheeled chair or moving clumsily on crutches, Anne retained her cheerfulness of spirit and her forthright turn of speech, maintaining a flow of correspondence with friends she had written to all her life, in Scotland, England and America.

In 1839 her son married. His young wife was a great comfort to Anne, but sadly this beloved daughter-in-law was to die too, only four years after the wedding. The letters to her many friends and acquaintances written over the last thirty-five years of her life were edited and published by her son a few years after her death. In them we find Anne's observations on the state of society and on the events of the time, along with glimpses of her own life, with its fulfilments and its sorrows. Her strong Christian convictions are expressed with the verve which appealed to her many readers.

Anne's love of nature never left her. She would have herself carried in a sedan chair to a nearby garden, sitting there for an hour or more, to breathe the scent of flowers and listen to bird-song. By now removed to a house in Manor Place, she took great delight in the view from her windows – trees, distant hills, the sky, the setting sun. She remained in good health during the last summer of her life, then, in October 1838, after a severe attack of influenza, she died aged 83. She is buried near the graves of four of her daughters in the churchyard of St Cuthbert's, Edinburgh. In the little churchyard at Laggan her memorial stone stands, beside that of her husband, who is buried there. In death they were not divided, for to each of them the place remained their 'ever-dear Laggan.'

CHAPTER 12

Women of the Clearances

A GENERATION OR SO after the suffering ensuing from the uprising of 1745 there were to be further times of hardship and distress for the erstwhile clansmen's families. Their former chiefs, those 'fathers' of the clans, were becoming landlords, their main interest no longer the well-being of their tenants but the profitability and 'improvement' of their lands. Increases in rent were inevitable, but could not be met. Many families were forced to move to the coasts or to remote hill areas so that the glens could be let to incoming flock-masters and their hordes of white-faced sheep. These men could pay.

The first thing the evicted tenants had to do was to build a house. A fore-sighted few had taken their roof-beams with them, which helped on the building, but the early days had to be spent as best they could, living in makeshift shelters, the old and infirm huddled under blankets. Cooking was done on fires of whatever material could be found.

On the coasts the women were expected to work at gathering and burning kelp. They had to learn to prepare meals from shell-fish and various forms of sea-weed. Many suffered illnesses from working in the wet, cold conditions and from eating food to which they were not accustomed. Their men, most of whom had never set eyes on the sea before, often lost their lives fishing off the rocks or in fragile boats. Those evicted to the remote uplands had to scratch to make fields out of the patches of grass among the heather. People who could raise the money for the fare emigrated to America or Canada. Some were despatched there, in ramshackle ships, by lairds anxious to be rid of penniless tenants. Conditions on board were appalling – men, women and children crammed below decks, in open bunks. Some women had to give birth in these conditions. Many died, babies and young children too, their bodies cast into the sea.

On arrival, those who survived the voyage found life even harder than in the remote hills or coasts of home. Huge trees had to be felled to build cabins and to make fields. There is scant record of what the women went through, but it can be imagined – camping in the woodland, while the cabins were being built, bitten by strange insects and snakes, guarding their children from attacks by bears and other unknown animals, lying listening to the howls of wolves in the night. The intense cold of the winters caused unimaginable suffering. In summer the humid heat made for sickness and exhaustion. The older generation were never to adapt to these conditions. Many women were left on their own as their men went off to seek work on established farms further inland, or to join the army of King George as a means of livelihood. For the women and children, merely surviving was a struggle.

In their native land the wild plants – leaves and roots – gave a certain amount of sustenance, but on this alien shore even the plants were strange. Berries and nuts, too, had to be tried out and to get 'sugar from the trees' was a skill that had to be learnt. The native American people were not unfriendly to the families, bringing their babies to a ceilidh round the fire on a winter night.

Meanwhile, back in the Highlands, protesters against the invading sheep were becoming active. Their protests were of course summarily dismissed, with the help of the military and threats of imprisonment. As time went on, however, gatherings were held, the rights of the lairds to withhold grazings and to increase rents were questioned, plans of action were discussed and formulated.

In 1881, eviction notices were served on the tenants of Braes, on Skye, who had refused to pay their rent until the hill grazing for their cattle was restored to them. The tenants burned the notices. The following April, one bitterly cold day at dawn, 50 policemen with Sheriff Ivory in tow, marched from Portree to Braes. Many of the men were away at the fishing so it was left to the women to resist. Their children beside them, they climbed to a vantage point on the hillside, their only weapons sticks and stones which they hurled at the police, injuring several quite severely and forcing the rest to retreat. A plaque at the roadside now commemorates this event. It is known as the Battle of the Braes. At this time, Màiri MacPherson from Skye was writing poems and songs exhorting the people to resist oppression, to defy the landlords, to claim their natural rights. She put heart into the people. Riots took place in many parts of the Highlands.

At last, in 1883, a Royal Commission was set up to look into the people's condition. Three years later an Act was passed which gave security of tenure to crofting tenants. Even after the passing of the Act the crofters of Glendale in north Skye were again besieged by police and Marines serving summonses. They were beaten off by the women, while the men, in defiance, drove the cattle into the hills.

By this time the landlords were finding another way to make their estates pay – by letting out large areas of land to 'sporting' tenants for the shooting of deer, grouse, almost anything that moved. This meant displacing more crofters and the building of lodges, even in remote places, for the accommodation of the sportsmen. These were wealthy people from the south or from overseas and enjoyed a high lifestyle with much entertaining. Some women from the crofts found employment in the lodges as cooks, cleaners, laundry-maids and so on, but the employment was only seasonal. It meant working long hours, in an alien environment, in some cases at a long distance from their homes and therefore without the support of their families.

Their day would start at 6am when they would carry pails of coal and jugs of hot water up the long stairways, and would not end till dusk, when the guests were, it was hoped, settled for the evening.

Language problems caused misunderstandings. Some young women suffered cruelty and abuse. Màiri MacPherson the poet, as we will see in the next chapter, knew what it meant to be falsely accused of theft, an unthinkable crime in the way of life to which she was accustomed. The clash of cultures inevitably brought distress and those who suffered were, of course, the minority.

CHAPTER 13

Great Màiri of the Songs
(1821–1898) – the Poet of Skye

MÀIRI MHÓR WAS BORN in 1821 in Skeabost, Skye, one of the family of John MacDonald, a crofter. She liked to call herself after her father – 'Màiri Nighean Iain Bhan' – Mairi, daughter of fair Ian. Later, she was to be known as 'Great Màiri of the Songs.' Her mother Flora was the daughter of Neil MacInnes, a crofter in Snizort.

Màiri's parents had spent the first twelve years of their married life in Glasgow, refusing to be lured to some unknown destination in Canada. Most of their children were born in Glasgow, except Màiri and one brother who were born in Skeabost after their parents' return to Skye. Here she grew up, leading the usual life of a crofter's daughter. She learnt to manage cattle, to help at the harvest and at the cutting of the peats, as well as acquiring all the domestic skills of cooking, baking, spinning, dyeing, and waulking the cloth. All the while she listened to and memorised the poems and songs of the people, songs which were sung at work as well as at the evening ceilidhs.

At that time every community had its bard, a poet who would record day-to-day happenings, would eulogise some person who deserved praise for some benefit he had bestowed, or, quite often, would denounce with satire some miscreant who had maligned people. These satires were dreaded. The public shame sometimes led to serious mental anguish. Poetry came naturally to the people, as a record of their experience of love, sorrow, joy. The poems, most of which were set to traditional music, were not often written

Carrying home the peats, Isle of Lewis, c. 1920

The 'herring girls'

St Clements Church, Rodil, Harris, where Mairi MacLeod is buried face down 'so that her tongue, which had uttered lies, would not point to heaven'

Flora MacDonald

Anne Grant of Laggan, from a miniature painted in her 69th year

'Waulking the Cloth', Eriskay

The Battle of the Braes, Skye, 1882

Màiri Mhór at the distaff
(courtesy of the Highland Folk Museum, Kingussie)

Monument to
Màiri Mhór

Bringing home peats, Isle of Lewis

Copy of *The Raising of the Regiment* by William Skeoch Cumming
(courtesy of the Gordon Highlanders Museum, Aberdeen)

Frances Tolmie

(Permission to use photograph granted by Taylor and Francis Publishers)

Isabel Frances Grant with friend out collecting
(courtesy of Colonel Grant of Tomatin)

Margaret Fay Shaw
(courtesy of Canna Archives)

Dr I. F. Grant in graduate
gown
(courtesy of Highland Folk
Museum, Kingussie)

Self-portrait
by Jemima Blackburn

Gathering Bracken at Roshven, 1865
by Jemima Blackburn

(both courtesy of Mr Alan Blackburn, Roshven Farm, Lochailort)

down. They were part of the great oral tradition, which included story-telling, genealogy, the exchanges of riddles. There was always music, of the clarsach, the bagpipe, the fiddle and later, the accordion. People were accustomed to memorising great numbers of poems and turning them into songs. Màiri became a prodigious collector and memoriser of these songs.

At the age of 27 she left Skye for Inverness, where she married Isaac MacPherson, a shoe-maker, whose people belonged to Skye. They had four children. Sadly, in 1871, Isaac died, it is thought of cholera or another of the infections prevalent at the time. To provide for her family, Mairi took work as a servant in a big house in the town. There, she was wrongly accused of stealing some of her mistress's clothes. Stealing had always been considered a disgraceful offence among people who had so few worldly goods. She was tried and imprisoned. The charge being read in English, she would never fully understand of what she was accused. Even the jailers upbraided her in English. This whole experience rankled harshly with her. The sense of humiliation led to personal outrage. To calm her mind during the long days of confinement she began to compose, discovering a gift which had lain dormant in her busy years. This is part of what she said of her predicament:

> It was the degree of harassment I suffered
> That put the edge on my nature
> And the oil of pain sharpened it...
> And tho' my poetry had never been heard
> The shame put it together.

She found her voice and from that time on she used it in praise of her people and her land and in defence of any form of attack on them. In what is perhaps her best known song 'When I was Young' she tells of the happiness of her early life in Skye:

Easement of sadness in early rising
on a May morning and I in Os
One to another the cattle calling
the dawn arising above the Storr
A spear of sunlight upon the mountains
saw the last shadow of darkness gone
The blithesome lark high above me singing
Brought back to mind days when I was young.

On release from prison Màiri went to Glasgow to train as a nurse in the Royal Infirmary there, as so many of her fellow islanders have done, before and since. She qualified as a nurse and obstetrician and practised in Glasgow and Greenock. By this time she must have acquired an ability to read, as well as to speak English. This was to be of help to her when she was to enter the world of politics in the fight for Land Reform in the Highlands. The emotional drive of her songs was an inspiration to all those concerned in the movement and drew her to the attention of John Murdoch, who transcribed and published some of them in the radical paper he founded – *The Highlander*. She also gained the friendship of Charles Fraser MacKintosh, a champion of the crofters, and canvassed with him in the election campaign, when he became an MP in 1874.

Though writing as an émigrée in the Lowlands, Màiri never lost an opportunity to come home to the Highlands, to Skye or Inverness, to keep in touch with things, attending meetings and ceilidhs. She was gregarious by nature and made many friends, among them Professor John Stuart Blackie, the Celtic scholar. She made a plaid for him in what became known as the 'Blackie tartan.' He always wore it and it was placed on his coffin when he died.

After rioting in Lewis, Skye and other places, the Crofters'

Act was passed in 1886. This gave people security of tenure in their holdings, but still did not give them access to the land they needed. Mairi continued to encourage them to defend their rights. In her poem 'Eilean a' Cheo' – 'Isle of Mist' she speaks of her longing to return to her homeland:

> Tho' trials great and sorrow
> My grey head now enshroud
> And my life's sun is setting
> Behind a darksome cloud
> Yet still I'm fondly longing
> O would the day were come
> To see my winged island
> My native Highland home.

In 1886 Màiri did indeed return to Skye. She had become the bard of the Land Reform movement, many of her poems appearing in the *Oban Times*. She was disappointed that many of the ministers of the Church of Scotland sided with the landlords during the time of the Clearances, due to the fact that under the custom of Patronage, the landlord had his say in the appointment of the parish minister. Some of the ministers of the Free Church which had broken away on account of Patronage also took the side of the landlords. She sang:

> The preachers have so little care
> Seeing the ill-treatment of my Isles' folk
> And so silent about it in the pulpit
> As if brute beasts were listening to them.

Màiri shows some inconsistency in that she maintains a certain respect for some of the 'uaisle' (nobility) who may have been guilty of cruelty. This probably stems from the immemorial feeling of regard for the chief, in spite of his failings, when he was the true father of the clan. Also, in Màiri's case, she was fortunate in having a fair-minded landlord in Skeabost. She celebrated the work of the Land Court which had been set up after the passing of the Crofters' Act and when a second Commission investigated the development of deer forests she felt optimistic enough to envisage the return of people to the Highlands.

Sorley MacLean, in a paper for the Gaelic Society of Inverness, writes that Màiri was, undoubtedly, the 'poet of the Clearances'. If her poems are often garrulous, they have an evocative lyrical quality and power. Her joie de vivre communicated itself to the people of whom she was so gloriously proud.

On her return to Skye Màiri was given, rent-free, Woodside Cottage in Skeabost by the benevolent proprietor Lachlan MacDonald. Here, she continued to compose songs and to attend meetings.

In 1891 her poetry was published in book form by her patron, Lachlan MacDonald, with illustrations arranged by William Fraser and an introduction by the scholar Alexander MacBain. John Whyte, a well-known authority on Gaelic, took down the poems from Màiri's recitation – 8–9,000 lines from memory: she could read her own work in print, but could not write it.

She died in 1898, in Portree, after a short illness, to be buried in Inverness, where her married life had been spent. The Provost and the Town Clerk met the funeral party from the Kyle train and a large crowd of sorrowing people followed the coffin to the Old Chapel graveyard. This was indeed the burial of a woman of renown. A memorial to Màiri was put up by Charles Fraser MacKintosh. The inscription reads:

Loving the Highlands and its people
Ever forward in their cause
By speech and song
She merited and received
The affectionate regard
Of Highlanders.

A plaque to her memory was unveiled at Skeabost in 1966 and a film of her life was made for television in 1998, to commemorate the centenary of her death.

Today, Màiri Mhór and her work are commemorated by the setting-up of a Màiri Mhór Gaelic Song Fellowship. This involves the teaching of her songs in schools and colleges throughout the Highlands and Islands. Many talented young singers have emerged. This would have rejoiced Mairi's heart, as would the progress of the Land Reform movement in recent years.

CHAPTER 14

A Woman's Work

TO KEEP HER FAMILY fed, clothed and nursed has always been a woman's work. How did she manage before the advent of the supermarket and the National Health Service? Not too badly, it seems, if we look back through the ages.

In the early years AD, the Iron Age, the family diet was a healthy one. Protein was there, from roe-deer or other game, killed by arrow or spear, or caught in traps, and in the speared or netted fish. Summer plants of many kinds would have provided sustenance and vitamin C from their roots, stems, leaves, buds, flowers and fruit. In autumn, families feasted on nuts and berries, much of which could have been dried and stored for winter. Hazel nuts contain more protein than eggs or cheese. Prehistoric middens provide proof of the amount consumed. And all this produce would, of course, have been strictly organic!

Silverweed was a much valued plant. The roots were dug up, dried and ground in the quern to make meal. In later times it became known as 'one of the seven breads of the Gael' and was so highly prized that places where it grew were allotted to different families. With its attractive silvery leaves and yellow flowers it is found all over the islands today.

Sorrel, with its slightly bitter taste, made a refreshing bite. The nodules on the roots of bitter vetch were dried and chewed, as gum is today, to ward off the pangs of hunger. This was a useful attribute in times of near famine. Seaweeds, particularly dulse and carrageen, with their content of iodine, made good eating for those on the coasts.

The dandelion, later to be known as St Bride's flower, as it comes out like a tiny sun at the time of her 'day' in early spring, has leaves, flowers and a root which can make salads and drinks. Today, it is grown commercially in New Jersey, USA, for its many properties.

Chickweed, on a slice of oatcake, made an appetising snack. In later times it was sold at markets, like watercress. As an infusion it induced sleep. Thyme and other herbs, also made healthy infusions.

The nettle was a valuable source of iron. It was made into soup along with some wild garlic, and was also rubbed on rheumaticky knees. The fibre made a kind of cloth. This use is just being rediscovered today. Alongside the nettle often grows the plant whose leaves relieve the sting of its neighbour – the docken. These leaves, when young and tender, can also be eaten.

Another close neighbour to the nettle is ground elder, or bishop weed, so called because the leaves grow in the shape of a mitre. It was often found near monasteries and was good for the treatment of gout.

Willowherb, or fireweed, makes a paradise for bees. In autumn, even in recent times, the dried leaves were made into an infusion resembling tea when the leaves from India and China were too expensive.

The plant which often symbolises the Highlands is the heather. It has had so many uses over the centuries, making bedding, thatching, rope, tea and ale. The Roman invaders, when they came north, tried many times to discover what made their Pictish enemies invincible, but the recipe for heather ale was kept rigorously guarded. Robert Burns is said to have enjoyed heather 'tea' and Robert Louis Stevenson wrote a poem on heather ale:

From the bonnie bells of heather
They brewed a drink lang syne
Was sweeter far than honey
Was stronger far than wine.

Today heather ale is brewed and drunk, whether from the original recipe or not.

Cooking facilities in the early years AD were basic. Meat and fish would have been cooked on a spit over the fire or in charcoal. A kind of unleavened bread would have been made on a hot stone in the embers.

Hot stones were also used to heat water or other liquids and were placed in wooden tubs to make a warm bath. Cauldrons were made of strips of bronze riveted together.

Heavy outdoor clothing, in early times, would have been made of deerskin, or the pelts of smaller mammals – badgers, otters, hares. Below this, men and women alike would have worn a tunic made of wool. A small upright loom, with the vertical strands weighted at the bottom by stone, and other strands pushed in horizontally, made fabric. These looms were still in use in the nineteenth century when the big horizontal looms came into use.

Later flax was grown to make a fine fabric – linen – of which the men's shirts were made. People of Celtic origin loved colour. The women were quick to find which plants they could use to produce the most beautiful dyes. Yellow for the shirts came from the stigmas of the crocus – saffron. Nettle gave a greenish yellow, sorrel gave red, corn – marigold and bog myrtle provided other shades of yellow, lady's bedstraw gave an orange red. Lichens and crotal on the rocks were highly prized for colouring fabrics of all kinds. Pots were kept busily boiling as the lengths of wool or linen were dipped in.

To make woollen yarn the women from the earliest times used the distaff and spindle. Spindle stones have been found on prehistoric middens. They could ply the distaff when walking about, perhaps herding livestock or on their way to the peat banks.

When spinning wheels were introduced in the late 18th century many women took badly to them, as it meant sitting to work. This could be pleasant enough, outside, by the door, on a summer day. But to sit meant somehow to be idle! Later, knitting became a walk-about job.

As the people gradually gave up their nomadic way of life and began to settle in small communities they could keep some livestock and grow crops. This meant that milk, butter, and cheese were added to their diet, along with oatmeal and bere meal made from barley. It is said that people thrive best on food which grows naturally in the part of the world where they live. So the Gaels owe their health and strength largely to the consumption of oatmeal. Taken in the morning as 'brose', raw oatmeal stirred with hot water, and, if liked, a little milk or honey, it was, and still is, a great provider of energy for the day ahead and, of course, is also made into porridge and oatcakes.

Trees are giant plants and have been a mainstay of people's lives the world over. In the Highlands of Scotland one tree has had a particular place in the lives of people there – the rowan. It is grown by the door of the house to protect the family from evil. Its berries, glowing red in the autumn sun, make a jelly, good as a relish with game, and a wine which is said to hold the secret of eternal youth.

As time went on cooking pots were made of iron and that great stand-by, the griddle, came into use. So broth – boiled vegetables, including nettles, with a little meat and barley – became a staple item of diet, as it is today. And on the griddle oatcakes, pancakes and scones were made.

In the early 18th century potatoes were introduced into the Highlands. At first the people were puzzled, thinking the not very attractive green tops were to be part of their diet, a new-fangled craze of the lairds. Then it was explained that it was the tubers which were edible. Thereafter of course, the potato took over, to such an extent that when the crop was blighted near famine ensued. Peas were tried, turnips came in, but nothing equalled the popularity of the potato.

When the 'improving' lairds of the 18th and 19th centuries planted many deciduous and ornamental trees to enhance their estates, the people were made to get rid of their goats as they damaged the lairds' fine new plantings. This deprived them of a valuable source of meat and milk. When the estates were developed for 'sport', that is, the commercialised killing of deer, grouse, partridge, pheasant, salmon and trout, the people lost what had always been considered their right; to take 'a deer from the forest, a salmon from the river'. Even to trap a rabbit was looked at askance.

At times like these the women had recourse to whatever alternative sources of nourishment could be found – silverweed, bog bean, gulls' eggs, calves blood mixed with oatmeal to make 'black puddings'. It was again a question of survival.

Today, when self-sufficiency is not what it was, the grocer's van or the supermarket provides essentials, with the exchange of money. Nutritionally the value of the goods is sometimes doubtful.

The curative properties of plants are many and various. The wonder is that the knowledge of them, acquired through a long process of trial and error, has been carried in the minds of women through so many centuries and that many of them are being rediscovered today.

The meadowsweet, queen of the meadows, the wild form of spirea, was used for treating fevers and headaches, much as we use aspirin today. It is said that the great Celtic hero Cu-chulainn was cured of a fever when bathed in meadowsweet. An infusion of the plant makes a healthy drink and the flowers produce a sparkling wine.

St John's Wort was used to help cure nervous disorders, such as melancholia. St Columba used it to lift the depression of a herd boy whose lonely job had got him down. An infusion of raspberry leaves was given to pregnant women. The tiny yellow tormentil was good for worming and the treatment of dysentery. Comfrey, known as the bone-setter, was spread on splints to help the healing process.

For heartburn a drink of hot sea-water was recommended, though perhaps not often taken. Whooping-cough responded to a drink of mare's milk. A decoction of hawthorn leaves is said to help sore throats and also to correct high, or low, blood pressure. Truly a magical plant, this! It was certainly venerated from early times.

So many plants have always been there, waiting to release their gifts. Coltsfoot, for instance, that lovely early flower, could be dried and smoked in a clay pipe, when tobacco was scarce or expensive. The smoke was said to help asthma sufferers. Sphagnum moss, gathered and dried in the sun, was highly absorbent and even antiseptic; it was used as a field dressing in the two world wars and has done valuable service as the first disposable nappy!

Bog myrtle was repellent to many forms of insect life, including the midge. A sprig was often worn on the bonnet and placed in a jar in the kitchen. It was also a 'strewing herb', scattered on the floor to make a fresh smell and to keep household pests at bay. Today the oil is being extracted experimentally, in the effort to find a real midge deterrent.

The pith of rushes made the wick of the cruisie lamp. Rushes or willow withies made baskets and creels. Marram grass could be woven on an upright loom to make screens, even inner doors. The lovely white flowers of bog cotton were stuffed into pillow-cases to make an easy sleep.

All this plant lore which women have treasured down the centuries is now being recorded, and the bright hope of the day is that many women of the Highlands, particularly the young, are looking again at their great inheritance and making sure of its survival. Conservation, do I hear you say? May everything grow at its own sweet pace, and be there to be gathered, with loving care, by the generations to come.

CHAPTER 15

Women Wage-Earners

DURING THE LATE 18th and the 19th centuries, a money economy was taking over the old way of self-sufficient living, and the daughters of crofting families began to look to the wider world where waged employment could be found.

Some went off, as their forebears had, to farms in the south to do the work they knew best – harvesting. Often they took their sickles with them. It was said that women found it easier than men to stoop low, working with the sickle. We remember Wordsworth's 'solitary Highland lass' who was 'o'er the sickle bending'. When the scythe came into use this was considered men's work and women took to binding the sheaves. The harvesting was hard work and the pay was not great, but it was enough to allow them the pleasure of buying a dress, perhaps a necklace or a ring. On the long walk home in the autumn days they would band together in small groups, wary of being waylaid, with their purses hidden fast under their plaids.

In the late 1800s, when the herring were plentiful, many young women would travel from the west coast to the east and even into England, to work at gutting fish. Some, even in their early teens, would work from 9 am till 3 or 4 the next morning, if the catch was good.

They worked at an incredible speed, up to the rate of 60 fish a minute, with salt in their cut fingers and no food break, only a snatched cup of tea.

The pay was not good and nearly half of it went on paying for lodgings, but there was companionship and fun. The island girls would sing Gaelic songs, as they did at home when working. In their spare time they would knit, as they had done at home.

In later years their pay was increased and a bonus could be earned for exceptional work. Conditions improved also. Salt herring was the mainstay of the people's diet during the winter. From the inland districts crofters would travel with horse and cart to Loch Hourn, in October, sleeping overnight under the cart, to bring back a load of herring sufficient for two or three families. Now, sadly the herring are scarce and refrigeration has taken over from the salt cure.

Some families, cleared from their homes in the glens, emigrated only as far as the towns and cities. In Inverness, over-crowding in poor housing conditions and lack of sanitation resulted in outbreaks of cholera in the mid 1800s. Some people travelled to Aberdeen and Dundee. In Glasgow, in particular, many found themselves in conditions even worse than those of the so-called 'New World'. The squalor of the slums where they found the only accommodation available, led to illnesses of all kinds among the children, tuberculosis and rickets being the most prevalent.

While the men went to look for work the women had to adapt to a totally strange way of life, with crime, drunkenness and even rape on their doorstep. Communication, even with would-be helpful neighbours, was difficult as most had not a word of English.

Some families, the fortunate ones, lived with relatives already in the city while trying to find a place of their own. For the destitute, as many were, relief organisations were set up, such as the Glasgow Northern Highland Benevolent Society and the Highland Strangers Friendly Society. The Reverend Norman MacLeod was active in seeing to the people's spiritual needs and the Gaelic Chapels kept the Highlanders together.

By the late 19th century women were finding work as 'folders' in printing works, and other semi-skilled jobs, as well as working as domestic servants. Their men became constables, or 'chair-men', that is, carriers of sedan chairs, porters, all jobs requiring strength which they had in abundance as long as they were fed. So conditions began to improve.

In 1910 a 'National Vigilance Committee' was set up to protect Highland girls coming to work in the cities. Members would meet the girls as they came off the trains and escort them to hostels.

Meanwhile back in the Highlands, families were adapting to life in the 'planned villages' which had been set up by Sir James Grant: one at Grantown-on-Spey and one at Lewiston at the entrance to Glen Urquhart, near Loch Ness. The idea was to lessen the rate of emigration by providing better conditions for displaced people. At Lewiston, named after Sir James's son Lewis, each house had an allotment of ground for the growing of potatoes and the keeping of poultry, perhaps even the grazing of a cow. The men could work as smiths, weavers, shoe-makers, tailors, though some found it irksome to work in a settled way. As Mrs Grant of Laggan put it: 'a Highlander never sits easy at a loom; 'tis like putting a deer in the plough.' For the women, a settled life must have been welcome and they could find paid work also, as seamstresses, laundry-maids and so on.

In the late 18th century the Commission for Forfeited Estates set up linen mills where girls were to be trained as spinners, working at the looms while the teacher read aloud to them from an 'improving' book. The older girls were allowed to take looms home with them. One such mill was set up at Invermoriston, but it was not a success. The growing of flax to provide the raw material was dying out.

In other places the women's skills in spinning, weaving and knitting, in fact the working of wool into fabric, was to be put on a commercial basis. The ladies of the castles, the lairds' wives, in a genuine attempt to provide an income for the people still working their crofts, were encouraging the women to produce socks which were always in demand for the army. Wool would be bought and distributed over a wide area and the socks subsequently collected and paid for.

Woven fabric, which came to be known as tweed, coloured by the beautiful natural dyes known to the women, was much in demand for warm clothing by the people coming up to hunt and fish in the Highlands, and in particular, cloth woven in the island of Harris became world famous.

Eventually an establishment known as 'Highland Home Industries' was set up for the selling of garments in the cities.

The money economy was slowly but surely encroaching even into the homes of the Highland people.

CHAPTER 16

A New Form of 'Fostering'

DURING THE TWENTIETH CENTURY a new responsibility fell largely on the shoulders of crofters' wives. This was the care and up-bringing of orphaned or under-privileged children from the cities – notably Glasgow and Greenock. This 'boarding-out' with crofters' families was considered a sound alternative to the insti-tutionalising of children. They were supplied with clothing and an allowance was made for their keep. Regular visits were paid by inspectors to check on their welfare.

The task of looking after these children, along with her own brood, was sometimes quite onerous for a crofter's wife. Children from difficult backgrounds were often awkward to manage. Some, transported from the crowded city streets to the wide spaces of the Highland hills became completely disorientated and tried to run away.

They were, of course, expected to do light work on the croft, before and after school – gathering sticks, fetching water, feeding livestock. These were strange tasks for city children and had to be learnt.

Much patience was needed by the crofting parents and by their children. But the old system of fostering was not long forgotten and in many cases close links were forged between families and their 'guests'. These 'guests' were soon speaking in the fluent Gaelic they heard all around them on the croft. The 'boarded-outs', as they came to be known, benefited greatly from living in the clean air, on a diet of fresh food. Their presence helped to keep the schools open in places where the numbers of native chil-dren were falling.

On leaving school some were reluctant to leave their adopted homeland and managed to find work locally. Some married into the family where they were brought up, or into a neighbouring family. This brought a welcome infusion of new blood into the place. Many of those who went away kept in touch with their 'foster' family over the years, coming back to visit and bringing tokens of thanks.

CHAPTER 17

A Highland Lady (1797–1882)

ANOTHER GRANT LADY, also a prolific writer, who produced her own version of *Letters from the Mountains* was Elizabeth Grant of Rothiemurchus in Badenoch, Strathspey.

A lady of the big house, but very down to earth, she has left us a memorable picture of the life and times of a Highland family during the nineteenth century. Thankfully we now have the full text of the story, which, when first published in 1898, some 13 years after the death of the author, had been edited and abridged by a niece.

Originally written to interest her children, the book immediately became a best-seller, and has remained so ever since. The story is told clearly, vividly, with fascinating detail, so that the reader is caught up in it and stays with it to the end. Remarkably, the events described had taken place many years before they were thus recorded.

Elizabeth was born in 1797, in a newly-built house in Charlotte Square, Edinburgh. Her father, John Peter Grant, and her mother, Jane Ironside, had married young, 'in their dancing days' as Elizabeth put it. Her mother was proud of her Saxon ancestry, her father of his descent from a clan chief. They started married life in Edinburgh, where John Peter practised law, spending their summers at the Doune, the Grant property in the Highlands. They entertained lavishly, as was the custom of the time.

After a few years, hoping to increase his income and with political ambitions simmering in his mind, her father moved the family to London, practising English law, and finding himself nearer to the seats of power. More children were born – Jane in 1800, then William, then Mary. The summers were still spent at the Doune, 'the spot on earth dearest to every one of us'.

A great welcome home always awaited them. When they first came, as a family, the people of the place were a little doubtful of the 'foreign lady' their 'little laird' had married. John Peter was small of stature and not handsome, but much loved. When his young wife was found to be a quick learner at spinning, dyeing wool, brewing beer and the other household skills practised in a Highland home, they soon took to her.

The Doune and its outlying small farms provided the young family with all the foodstuffs they needed. The hunters and fishers could supply game, venison, rabbits, hares, salmon and trout. The forest was a source of income as timber fetched good prices during the wars with France.

For the children the place was paradise. They had the freedom to roam the moors, picking blueberries and brambles, climbing trees, splashing in the burns. Elizabeth later described herself at this time as 'a tall, pale, slight, fair child to look at, but I seldom ailed anything.'

Their education was not neglected. John Peter made sure they had tutors and governesses, he himself insisting on discipline and taking time to read aloud to them from Shakespeare, Milton, and other classical works. And they had, he said, 'to learn Highland life again' after having been long in England.

They still spent time in the south, with relations of their mother, but from 1812, their home was to be the Doune, though their father had to be away from time to time, on legal or political business. Fearing an invasion by the French he, like other Highland lairds, had recruited men into a home guard, the Fencibles.

Elizabeth revelled in getting to know all the many cousins,

uncles, aunts, distant relations and neighbours who made up the Rothiemurchus community, hearing the legends and learning the long history of the clan.

At nearby Kinrara, where Jane Maxwell, the Duchess of Gordon, had made a 'guest house' where the literati from all over the country could stay to enjoy hunting and fishing, music and dancing, the Grants and all the neighbouring lairds' families were always welcome.

Elizabeth enjoyed these visits. Aged 15, she was an accomplished young woman, well read, fluent in French, playing the clarsach, a Highland harp. She helped her father to catalogue books in a library he was setting up. About this time she began keeping a journal. This was to be useful for her later on.

Soon it was time for her to make her début in society by attending the 'Northern Meeting' in Inverness. This social occasion had been set up by the Duchess of Gordon and continued well into modern times. It consisted of a week-long gathering of families from all over the Highlands, with hunting for the men, outings for the women and balls in the evenings. Elizabeth's entrée was deemed a success.

Two years later, when John Peter's overspending on attempts to gain a seat in Parliament necessitated a return to practise at the Bar, the family had to move to Edinburgh. Here, Elizabeth suffered real personal sorrow. She and a friend of her brother William had fallen deeply in love, but, on account of a bitter quarrel between her father and the young man's father, the match was forbidden. Sorrow bore hard on her sensitive nature, and Elizabeth became quite seriously ill.

By 1820 the financial position of the family was such that William was forced to give up his legal studies and to come north to manage the estate for profit. There was a humiliating 'execution' in the house, when goods were seized on account of serious debts. Their mother now being often ill or indisposed, the three girls took over the running of the house. Costs were reduced wherever possible. Even firing being economised, Elizabeth became ill from sleeping in a damp bed. She and her mother did not go to the celebrations for the visit of King George IV to Edinburgh. John Peter presented a casket of the special Glenlivet whisky and 50 brace of ptarmigan to his Majesty.

At this time Elizabeth was reading a lot and had started writing essays, stories, even a novel. On a journey to Edinburgh she travelled for the first time, in order to economise, in a public carriage and found it 'very disagreeable'.

Her brother William was imprisoned for a short time in the Calton gaol in Edinburgh for debts incurred during his extravagant student days. He also took on his father's debts of £60,000. Jane found a wealthy husband and was married quietly at the Doune.

At Rothiemurchus 'poultry, the garden and the river' kept the household supplied. Shopkeepers in Inverness would not honour orders on account of unpaid bills. Surplus produce – eggs, wool, fruit – was sold to the shooting lodges in the neighbourhood.

The situation was precarious. In desperation Elizabeth and Mary set to trying to make some money by writing. They worked in the long winter evenings in an attic room where they managed to keep a fire burning and caught in pails the rainwater coming through the roof! A story sent to *Blackwood's Magazine*, with high hopes, was not even acknowledged. A publication called *The Inspector* paid £3 for a contribution. Subsequently they received £40 for further efforts. This was a fortune and went far beyond the buying of much needed shoes!

Their father lost his seat in Parliament but he was knighted and awarded a judgeship in Bombay, perhaps on account of the whisky and ptarmigan! The Doune, that once happy family home, was to be let to shooting tenants. All the family possessions were sold, only the furnishings left. As Mary said, 'we are done with home,' as they set sail on a four month voyage to India.

After a trying period of acclimatisation in this new continent Elizabeth managed to resume some of her former activities, going riding in the cool of the morning with her father. On some of these rides they were accompanied by Colonel Smith, an Irishman, a cavalry officer with the East India Company. Soon he was coming often to dine with the Grants. He arranged a camping trip, took members of the family for drives in the evenings. So it was that he and Elizabeth came to know each other well and in 1829 they were married. A year later their daughter Janey was born.

Sadly, the colonel suffered quite severely from asthma, a condition which was to plague him for the rest of his life. It was decided then that he should retire and return with his family to his native clime at Baltiboys, in County Wicklow, 20 miles south of Dublin. As Elizabeth put it in her *Memoirs*: 'then indeed I felt I was gone out from among my own kindred and had set up independently – a husband, a baby and an end to Eliza Grant.'

Yet it was far being an end. It was to be the beginning of a new life in her adopted country, which she was to chronicle later in another volume, *The Highland Lady in Ireland*. Finding her husband's land in a state of neglect, she set about helping him to make improvements in draining, in adopting new methods of cultivation, in bettering the housing conditions of the tenantry, in setting up schools. These were all aspects of estate management that she had had experience with at Rothiemurchus. The schools project was one in which she was particularly involved. Education, she considered, was of primary importance in the building up of a better quality of life for the people.

A second daughter, Annie, was born in 1832 and six years later, a son, Jack. Through the years of child-bearing and rearing Elizabeth kept the struggle for improvement of things at Baltiboys going. And she kept abreast of the political movements of the time, as the trenchant observations in her writings show. She also reduced the costs of their life-style where possible.

Then, in 1843, in order to retrench, they decided to let the house and policies, to sell the riding horses and to live in France for a time. They went first to Pau where, it was hoped, the colonel's health would improve, then to Avranches in Normandy.

It was during her time of comparative leisure here that Elizabeth began writing her *Memoirs*, as she puts it, 'begun to please my children and my niece.' She also kept a journal and recorded her stay in France, her journeys around the country and her observations of the people. She found the peasants happier than those in Ireland, but she did not enjoy the society of the British émigrés she found there. All this eventually became another volume, *A Highland Lady in France*.

Sadly, her beloved sister, Mary, who had been ailing, died in France. 'I am lonely without her', Elizabeth wrote. They had shared so much – happy childhood days, later times of anxiety, the thrill of having their first writings published.

Returning to Ireland in 1845 they found famine looming. 'It is in frightful reality to be seen in every face', Elizabeth writes. She set up soup kitchens, gave out rice and milk and visited all the tenants. Dysentery, influenza and other illnesses were prevalent among the people. Those who could raise money for the fare emigrated to America.

Elizabeth, though deeply worried by the situation at home, and by the troubles her father and brother William were experiencing in India, managed somehow to keep on with her writing.

Her work was published by William and Robert Chambers in their *Edinburgh Journal*. Her stories and essays were much appreciated and the money she received was welcome. It helped to relieve some of the famine conditions and to keep her beloved school open.

She kept in touch with the political and literary events of Britain and of Ireland and maintained a social life for the family. Her daughters married. Her son, Jack, sadly died. Eventually her dear Colonel Hal succumbed to the affliction that had worn him down. Elizabeth lived out her last years alone, dying at 85.

Though she had spent many years in Ireland she was always 'of Rothiemurchus'. She has left us this unique record of life on a Highland estate, in France and in rural Ireland, written with wit, clarity and wisdom.

CHAPTER 18

Jane Maxwell, Duchess of Gordon (1749–1812) – 'The Flower of Galloway'

JANE MAXWELL DID A great deal to make Highland culture popular and fashionable among the nobility. Known in her youth as 'the flower of Galloway', that lovely land where the Gaelic came ashore, across the Irish Sea, Jane was a famous beauty. She encouraged the spread of literature and music from the North into Edinburgh and even London, and became a symbol of Highland vivacity that endured even after her death.

Jane's father, Sir William Maxwell, and her mother Magdalene (née Baird) having separated early in Jane's life, she and her mother and two sisters went to live in a tenement in the Old Town of Edinburgh. Here, Jane and her younger sister Betty, boisterous girls, soon grew beyond control, playing wild games with the local children, jumping on to the backs of pigs which roamed the narrow streets, and riding in travellers' carts. In one of these mad exploits Jane lost the forefinger of her right hand.

As she entered her teens she became almost the 'adopted' daughter of a friend of the family, the judge Henry Home, Lord Kames. Attracted to this lively 13-year-old, and a believer in education for girls, he encouraged her to read and gave her the use of his library. She also took lessons in drawing and singing. Thus began her lifelong interest in literature and music.

At the age of 17 Jane became engaged to a young army officer of the Black Watch, a member of the Fraser family. He was sent to fight in America and was soon reported missing, presumed dead. In 1767 Jane met Alexander, 4th Duke of Gordon, at a ball in Edinburgh. The somewhat reserved, handsome young man of 24 fell in love with the lively beauty and later that year they were married. It is said that soon after the wedding Jane received news from her former suitor that he was about to return home to marry her. Her grief was overwhelming and may well have been the underlying cause of the subsequent tempestuous relationship with her Duke.

Her father and her good friend Lord Kames, knowing her wild ways, both wrote to her at this time, proffering advice as to seemly behaviour in her new role. She was certainly unconventional in manner and speech with a great sense of humour and careless of her reputation.

At Gordon Castle, in Aberdeenshire, a gaunt, fortified tower house, she entered with gusto into her duties as chatelaine, supervising accounts, seeing to the moral and religious education of the servants, looking after tenants and always finding time to listen to problems.

During the following ten years the Duke had the castle extended, with pavilions and ornamental gardens made. When it was considered that the village of Fochabers was too near to their now grandiose abode they simply had it removed!

Jane had her own small summer house and a garden at Quarry Wood, with unusual trees and shrubs. She was an early riser and liked to take a ride before breakfast to her 'shrubbery'. She also went bathing in the North Sea, even in the coldest weather.

Meanwhile, children were arriving at regular intervals – Charlotte in 1768, then George, Madelina, Susan, Louisa, Georgina, Alexander. Nine natural children of the Duke were also brought up at the castle.

Gordon Castle during these years was a lively place, full of comings and goings, with laughter and music everywhere. The butler, William Marshall, was a talented fiddler and composer. Encouraged by Jane, he published his *Strathspeys and Reels*. He also composed reels specially to celebrate occasions in the life of the family.

After the birth of her last child, Alexander in 1785, Jane and the Duke lived for a time at their house in Edinburgh, where she immersed herself in the doings of the literary world. Here, the young Robert Burns was introduced to her. She invited him to her supper parties, where the latest books were discussed, and the following year he visited her at Gordon Castle. Jane had the perception to recognise his great talent. With her Scottish voice, her lively speech and her charisma she would have inspired the poet and helped set him on his way to future greatness.

By now Jane was becoming a toast in London society, giving suppers and balls when she went south for 'the season.' She brought William Marshall to provide Highland music as she danced her lively steps, wearing a dress of tartan taffeta.

Becoming involved in politics, she canvassed for William Pitt the Younger, who was much impressed by her thinking and ability.

Now it was time to start 'marrying-off' her daughters, an enterprise in which no effort was spared. Three of the daughters married dukes, one a marquess. Her youngest daughter Georgina she took to Paris in 1802 when the treaty of Amiens had ended the war with France. Here, at a dinner presided over by Napoleon and Josephine, Jane made a spectacular entry, seating herself on the Emperor's right. Her idea was to marry Georgina to Josephine's son Eugene Beauharnais. But there she had no success, Napoleon having other ideas for his step-son. Georgina was subsequently married to the Duke of Bedford.

Jane now got busy organising the most fashionable event in the social life of the Highland élite – the Northern Meeting. As distances between communities in the north were long and roads, if they existed, extremely rough, it was planned that people should be invited to gather in Inverness in mid-October when harvests were over, and stay there for about a week to socialise. As well as the aristocracy many professional people would attend – doctors, lawyers, provosts and merchants. No politics or business affairs were to be discussed.

Each day, in the mornings, the men would go out for a bit of sport – fishing or shooting – while the women could visit friends or look at goods for sale. After an early evening dinner in one of the inns the fun would begin – dancing in the big hall at the Town House. A few might prefer to play cards, but the ball was the great thing. Reels, jigs, Strathspeys, Highland dances of all kinds were enjoyed with gusto. Duchess Jane would be in her element. At midnight tea and coffee were served. Next morning breakfast would be taken at the inn and the day would be repeated to everyone's delight. This 'Northern Meeting' was held until recent times in Inverness, often with one of the 'Royals' attending.

In 1791, when her son, the Marquess of Huntly, was recruiting for the Gordon Highlanders, Jane set out to help him in the process. Riding a white horse and wearing a black feather bonnet with her tailored outfit, she held 'the King's shilling', a golden guinea, between her teeth, offering it thus to the men so that they could say that they had 'kissed a Duchess.' The success of this particular ploy has not been recorded, but no doubt it was considerable.

To celebrate the revival of the tartan – the wearing of which had been prohibited for 40 years after the rebellion of 1745 – Jane had Black Watch tartan woven. She herself dressed overall in Black Watch tartan taffeta at a London ball. Her popularity was such that Highland dress, music and dancing became fashionable, even at Court.

By now the Duke was finding it impossible to keep pace with Jane's lifestyle. He retreated into his own ways, looking after the estate and finding a new love in the daughter of his housekeeper. He and his Duchess went their separate ways.

Jane declared in a letter to an old friend, 'I am going to build a shieling at Badenoch' and this is what she did, at Kinrara, just south of Aviemore. Here, she and her daughter Georgina lived very simply in an old farmhouse enjoying, as she had always done, the freedom and fresh air. In earlier days she had followed the precepts of the French philosopher Jean Jacques Rousseau, taking her children out to the wild country whenever possible, to run about barefoot, becoming the familiars of birds, beasts, flowers.

Elizabeth Grant of Rothiemurchus, a neighbouring estate, remembered how Jane converted a barn into a place for lady visitors to stay and a stable for the men. Very soon her many friends from London and elsewhere were flocking to this retreat in the hills, where the Duchess entertained in her usual style, with vivacity and wit. There was music and dancing after long days spent in the open air.

With the number of visitors increasing year by year, Jane built a new house a little further up the River Spey. This was an unusual house for the day, the many windows filling it with light. It had nine guest bedrooms. Jane's son, the young Marquess of Huntly, was often with her, entertaining the company with much of his mother's charisma.

Inevitably, money problems began to surface. The Duke was in debt. Jane had to press for a settlement. The death of her younger son Alexander at the age of 23 brought great sadness, but in spite of sorrow and financial stress she remained active and forward-looking. She had an extension built on the house at Kinrara and bought large quantities of shrubs and trees, 100 larches and 50 mountain ash, her great loves. These trees are still flourishing today and the house is lived in. Kinrara was her home, yet the hankering for London persisted.

In the early 1800s, despite failing eyesight, she was on the move again, visiting her daughters, dancing at balls. When on her own in London, her finances now at a very low ebb, she was obliged to stay in lodgings or in wretched hotels. In April 1812, in a small hotel in Piccadilly, she fell ill. Her children and her Duke all rushed to her side. She died, peacefully, aged 63.

She was buried, as she had requested, at Kinrara, among her beloved trees. She lies in consecrated ground, the site of an ancient chapel. On her tombstone – a huge block of marble – are inscribed, as she had wished, the names and marriages of all her daughters. Above stands an obelisk of granite.

CHAPTER 19

Frances Tolmie (1840–1927) – 'A Woman Nobly Planned'

TWO WOMEN WHO WERE later to collect, and sing, many of the songs of the Islands were Frances Tolmie and Margaret Fay Shaw.

Frances was born in 1840 at Uiguish Farm, across the loch from Dunvegan Castle in Skye. The Tolmies had been in Dunvegan since the sixteenth century. They were a sept of the ancient MacLeods of Gairloch.

Frances's father died young. Her mother, who came from the island of Eigg, was left with 5 sons and 4 daughters to bring up. Hugh MacAskill, her mother's brother, who had a large farm, became the guardian of the family. He and his wife were in the habit of entertaining a large circle of literary friends from many places. This made a congenial atmosphere for Frances's early years.

One older brother had emigrated to New Zealand, and by the time she was 14 another brother, John, had become a minister, with a church on the mainland at Strontian. She and her mother, with sister Mary and brother Alan, went to live with John at his manse there. Here, Fanny (as she was known in the family) had lessons from a teacher from Edinburgh and also learnt to play the piano.

Soon however, it was back to Skye when her brother got a living at Bracadale. The village schoolmaster would visit the house and read to the children and sing Gaelic songs. This inspired Fanny, who made a great effort to learn Gaelic so that she could write down the words of the songs. At this time, aged 16, she was described as tall, blue-eyed, with long red-gold hair.

A Miss Matilda Wrench, a London woman who was working with the Ladies Highland Association in the setting-up of schools in the Highlands, encouraged Fanny to spend a winter in Edinburgh, where she studied French and Italian and also music. She was befriended by the Constable family, the well-known printers and publishers. Back in Skye she returned to the study of Gaelic, basing her reading on the Gaelic Bible.

Around the mid-nineteenth century, efforts were being made to find some form of employment, preferably home-based, for the women of the crofts. Their skills in spinning, weaving and knitting were well-known. The MacLeod chief's sister arranged an order for a thousand pairs of socks to be knitted for a Highland regiment. She got Fanny to help distribute the wool, collect the socks and pay the workers. This was to involve long walks over rough and lonely terrain, to reach the various crofts. Her mother insisted that she be accompanied on these outings. Uighrig (Effie) Ross became her companion, a woman whom she later remembered as:

> rather feeble-minded in practical life, but with a poetical soul… a kind creature, but wild-looking and apt to turn crazy if unduly provoked; she had immense front teeth, tawny locks of hair strayed from beneath her cap over a high and peaked forehead, and her old skirts hung in fringed tatters over her bare feet.

But Effie sang and told stories.

One of Effie's songs told of the 'Battle of Millegaraidh' in 1570, a battle at Waternish when the MacLeods inflicted losses on the MacDonalds of Clanranald. Effie knew all the words of this long tale. Her memory, like that of so many of her contemporaries, was phenomenal.

Fanny's Gaelic was now equal to the task of writing down the words of Effie's wonderful store of song. Traditionally, these had been handed down the generations in oral form. Fanny was now trying to use her musical skills in transcribing the tunes also.

Alexander Carmichael, the excise officer, who often visited her brother at the manse, encouraged her in her work. He was later to become a famous collector of all the folklore of the islands, as we have seen. Fanny herself was now becoming a real collector, listening avidly to all the singers who came about. Margaret Gillies sang several songs composed by Mary MacLeod, the 17th century poet, who was bard to the chief. Uighrig Beaton, another singer, whose mother had been a servant in one of the big houses visited by Johnson and Boswell during their Highland journey, told how the great man drank 18 cups of tea at breakfast!

Fanny's collection of songs (and stories!) was growing steadily when, in 1862, she went off again to Edinburgh with Matilda Wrench. Here, she got a post as governess to the daughters of the Constable family. Thomas Constable's library was a great joy to her. Here she found the *West Highland Tales* of Campbell of Islay, the *Book of the Dean of Lismore* and the lays of the Fiann, all the history and legend she could have wished for.

In 1863 her uncle Hugh, who had done so much for the family, died. Three years later Matilda Wrench also died. She left Fanny a legacy: 'all my books in Scotland and my writing table and... the sum of one hundred pounds sterling,' This was a goodly sum at that time.

Fanny returned to Skye, joining her mother and her sister Mary in Portree, then going on to her brother's manse at Contin, where she was to teach his children. They had a nurse from Skye who sang Gaelic lullabies and 'puirt a beul' (mouth music), to the delight of Fanny as well as the children.

Mary MacPherson (Màiri Mhór), big Mary of the songs, came to Contin 'in great trouble, to be comforted.' This would have been when she was wrongly accused of theft. She also sang for Fanny.

Her collecting was going well, but Fanny still had a hankering for further study. She kept in touch with her friends in Edinburgh and heard of developments in education, though, sadly, the University there did not yet accept women students. So, now 33 years old, she enrolled at Merton Hall, Cambridge, using the money Miss Wrench had left her. She stayed only two terms, studying and sometimes singing in Gaelic to the other students. She was to be well remembered both for herself and her wonderful long red-gold hair. 'She had the remoteness and greatness and simplicity of a dedicated spirit,' wrote a friend later, in her obituary.

Returning home, she accepted an invitation to spend a fortnight at Coniston in the Lake District, with a friend she had met in Edinburgh – Miss Harriette Rigbye. Miss Rigbye was a lady of private means with a gift for water-colour painting. The fortnight was gradually extended to weeks, months and longer as Fanny became the companion of her hostess, spending the summer in the Lake District and the winters in the south of France. At Coniston she met and enjoyed the company of John Ruskin.

In 1894 Miss Rigbye died, after a short illness. She made Fanny her heir, leaving her some £4,000, a sum which was to provide her with an income for the rest of her life. Fanny then joined her sister Mary in Oban, their mother having died a few years previously. With them they had Mary Ross from Skye. With Gaelic in the kitchen Fanny gradually awoke from 'the deep slumber in England'.

Things were moving in the Gaelic world. A chair of Celtic had been established at Edinburgh University. In 1871 the Gaelic Society of Inverness had been formed, the quality of its lectures making it almost a 'university of the north'. In 1892 the Gaelic Association held the first Mod at Oban, a celebration of Gaelic music, song and dance, on the lines of the Welsh Eisteddfod.

Fanny rejoiced in all these manifestations of interest in Gaelic culture and she was now able to buy the books she loved. She was back to her old ways of noting down songs, especially those sung to her by Mary Ross. She treasured her ever-growing collection but, not greatly valuing her own abilities, was always willing to pass on words and tunes to others. Then, in 1895, she was invited to contribute to *The Gesto Collection of Highland Music*, a collection compiled and arranged by Dr Keith Norman MacDonald, dedicated to the MacLeods of Gesto. Fanny gave Dr MacDonald some 45 songs. He was grateful for her help, but she was not entirely happy with his way of arranging the songs.

About this time Fanny renewed her acquaintance with Alexander Carmichael. Now retired and living with his family near Oban, he was busily putting together his own collection of folklore. One day, visiting the Carmichaels, Fanny met a young minister, a Celtic scholar from Sutherland, Dr George Henderson. He was thrilled to hear her sing old unpublished songs and urged her to write down the tunes. This she diligently did, adding notes and indexing the work.

During these years, Fanny listened to the songs Mary Ross remembered hearing sung by her grandfather and her father as they sat twisting heather into ropes and 'crooning' at the fireside on winter evenings. These were all duly recorded in notebook with pencil and the collection was sent to Dr Henderson. However, she was to hear nothing from him for a considerable time.

In 1905 Fanny and her sister Mary, with Mary Ross, moved to Edinburgh, where the Carmichaels were now also living. Here they enjoyed a pleasant social life. A few years later she received a visit from Miss Lucy Broadwood, honorary secretary of the Folk-Song Society, with a suggestion belatedly given by Dr Henderson. Eventually, to great acclaim, in 1911, Fanny's collection of traditional Gaelic songs, with the words and music faithfully transcribed, was published in a special edition of the *Journal of the Folk-Song Society*.

Some years previously, in 1909, when Marjory Kennedy Fraser's *Songs of the Hebrides* had been published, Fanny had generously sent songs to her which she included in the collection. Though Marjory's songs with adaptations and translations and piano accompaniment made quite attractive listening to drawing-room audiences, they did not have the realism of the authentic songs and singers known to Fanny and her fellow Gaels.

After the death of her sister Fanny returned to Skye to live in a small house she called Kilchoan, near Dunvegan, from where she could look across at the house of Uignish, where she was born. There she was visited by relations and friends of former days. She corresponded with many people. And she sang.

In 1924 she was elected an honorary member of the Royal Celtic Society, for services to Gaelic learning. She was among the very few women so honoured and she felt this was a great privilege. It was certainly due recognition of all her years of patient work.

On New Year's Eve in 1927, a wet and stormy night, hearing the wailing of a cat on the roof, she opened the sky-light of her bedroom to let the creature in. She fell and broke her leg. Complications set in and she did not recover. So, in the early days of the new year 'the grand old lady of Skye' was laid to rest at Duirinish, beside her father.

Of her work she said: 'All my songs have been learned just within the innocent circle of my home duties and are a true remnant of an early time.'

An appreciation in the *Oban Times* said of her that she was 'a lady of distinguished presence and charming manners, a woman nobly planned. When the eye saw her, it blessed her.'

CHAPTER 20

Margaret Fay Shaw (1903–2004) – A Gael by Adoption

A COLLECTOR WHO CAME later on the scene but whose aspirations were very similar to those of Frances Tolmie was Margaret Fay Shaw.

She was born in Philadelphia, of American parents, which makes her, of course, an American. But many an American has looked back to his or her roots and found them still healthily growing. So it was with Margaret, who was to become a true Scottish Highlander.

Her great, great grandfather John Shaw had come to Philadelphia from Scotland in 1782 with his four sons and had been given a large grant of land. His grandson Thomas, in the low-lying valley of Pine Creek built a house of brick and a factory, making sickles, hoes and ploughs for the incoming settlers. He also built a church and called the place Glenshaw.

There Margaret was born in 1903, the youngest of five daughters. She had a happy country childhood, playing in the creek, in the barn and in the apple orchard.

Her father Henry was a civil engineer, head of the family Foundry. He was well read, and Samuel Johnson was his idol. Her mother, Fanny Maria, was a 'Yankee' from Vermont, with English ancestors. Sadly, she died when Margaret was seven years old. The family then moved to a suburb of Pittsburgh.

At the age of 12 Margaret was learning to play the piano, a passion which was to last till the end of her life. When her father died, the family house was sold and she was sent to the boarding-school her sisters had attended. She was not happy there but, to her great delight, it was decided that she should go to school in Scotland, along with the daughter of a family friend. This school, St Bride's, was at Helensburgh on the firth of Clyde. Her teachers found her a slow learner, without much power of concentration, though musically gifted. In later life she was to receive honorary degrees from four universities: from St Francis Xavier's College, in Nova Scotia, from the National University of Ireland, then Aberdeen and Edinburgh.

At St Bride's her only disappointment was that she was to learn so little about Scotland – no Scottish history, nothing about the Gaelic language, no music. Then, one day, she heard for the first time, the pipes being played by 'a tinker at the kitchen door!' Thrilled, she rushed out to give him a penny. That was her intro-duction to the music of Scotland.

One evening, Mrs Kennedy Fraser, who was a collector of songs of the Highlands, came, with her sister and her daughter, to sing at the school. Margaret listened with avid attention. But, instinctively, she realised this singing was not authentic. The piano accompaniment, the conventional modes, turned the songs into drawing-room entertainment. But the sound had lit a spark in her, a spark that would light her on her long way to find the source of the music she had heard.

In summer she had a short stay in the Highlands, at Boat of Garten, returning by the Caledonian Canal to Oban and thence to New York. Here, she studied the piano and did odd jobs to make enough money to return to Scotland. When she finally reached Portree in Skye, she heard open-air psalm-singing, with a precenter, in traditional style. This, at last, was authentic Gaelic singing. Hearing it must have been a real inspiration.

Two years later, Margaret visited Scotland again with a friend, in the Islands of Barra, Eriskay, then Lewis and Harris and the Uists, travelling on bicycles. Then it was back to London and on to France.

She was still working at her piano and for a while lived a somewhat Bohemian life, with a sister, in Paris. Her driving impulse to discover and record the music of the Gael never left her. She managed to make a short stay in Ireland, where she met a collector of songs.

About this time she began to develop severe rheumatism which meant having to give up her professional piano-playing. This was a blow but she had other things on her mind. Though her family was against it, she set off again to the islands to collect the songs she loved. South Uist was the place she had fallen in love with. Here, she heard Mairi MacRae singing and knew at once she had found what she was looking for.

Mairi and her sister Peigí worked in the big house at Boisdale. They lived in a small traditional house and had a small croft. After hearing Mairi sing Margaret knew she had to see this woman again, to hear her sing, to find where she lived, how she lived, she and her sister and their families and friends. She soon found the house, asked if she could stay there whilst Mairi taught her to sing, and was given a warm welcome.

Eventually, Margaret was to stay there four winters and six summers, taking part in the work of the household and of the croft, looking after the sheep, baking oatmeal, making butter. She was also learning Gaelic, listening to the songs, recording the music and the words. She was also doing another kind of recording, with her camera. This was a heavy, old-fashioned affair, weighing 10 lbs. As she was tiny, carrying it around was a laborious task. She used it to great effect and to the amazement of the people who had never seen themselves in photographs before.

To augment her small income Margaret managed to sell several photographs to publications, including some to illustrate an article on South Uist for the *National Geographic Magazine*. Then, becoming ambitious, she put together a collection of songs, stories, recipes, cures; all the cultural lore of the island which, eventually, she had published as a book – *Folksongs and Folklore of South Uist*.

Her friend Fred Gillies, from whom she had learnt much of the history of the island, and who had encouraged her in her collecting, wrote a Gaelic poem in praise of her book; 'an ember was dying, she blew on it and brought it to life.' This book went into three editions and is still in print.

At an international folk music conference in Venice in 1949 her recordings were well received and in 1956 several songs were included in the Bartók memorial volume. This was to be her future accolade.

Meanwhile, with the urge to further her experience of the islands, their music and their life, she sailed to St Kilda, where the people were in a poor state and not much music was forthcoming. Then she went to the Aran Islands, off the coast of Galway, where she heard wonderful stories as well as songs. And the flowers growing in the limestone cracks! She sailed round the islands in curraghs and listened to Pat Mullen, teller of folk tales.

One strange experience occurred when she had to stay alone for three days on the uninhabited island of Mingulay, off Barra. She had gone there with a sheep farmer and three shepherds to photograph the high cliffs, where thousands of sea-birds nested. With them they had two nanny-goats as a milk supply. On arrival the goats ran off and could not be caught. Margaret, nothing daunted, volunteered to stay on the island, to catch and milk the goats, while the others went further.

The pipers of South Uist were famous. They had pipe-major John MacDonald of Inverness as their teacher. Margaret was privileged to be invited to sit in at some of his lessons in the Lochboisdale Hotel. She would play the piano for the pipers. One evening a young man came into the room. He was introduced as young Campbell of Inverneill. After some preliminary talk about music he said to Margaret, 'I hear you take photographs and I would like some for a book that Compton MacKenzie and I are writing.'

A few months later John Campbell asked her to join some friends he was inviting to Northbay, in Barra, where he had a house. This she did, enjoying walks with her host along the shore, walking in silence while he wandered off to catch butterflies, in which he was passionately interested. So she got to know John Campbell and his ways.

In 1935 he came over to America and stayed at Glenshaw, where Margaret was living to work on the book which was to become *The Book of Barra*, well known today. The evening before he was due to return to Scotland, he and Margaret went for a walk together and he asked her to marry him. She was taken aback, as during his stay, he had not shown the slightest interest in her. However, all went well and they were married, in Glasgow, in the manse of John's friend Calum MacLeod. The proceedings were in Gaelic. It was all very quiet and serious.

They spent their honeymoon in the Lofoten Islands and the Vesteraalens off the coast of Norway, where John studied the fishing and found that the problems of the fishermen were similar to those of the Hebrideans.

The next six weeks they spent aboard a motor yacht in mostly stormy weather. This was not conducive to John's writing and Margaret was glad when they came ashore at Northbay in Barra.

Here, they moved into a small corrugated iron house, as tenants of 'the Coddy', John MacPherson, postmaster and shopkeeper. He was a teller of folk tales, which were to become a book, *Tales told by the Coddy*.

With money given to her by her uncle George, Margaret bought a grand piano which they managed to squeeze into the little house. She and Compton MacKenzie's wife Faith played duets together. The piano was still her great love. She was not very attracted to MacKenzie himself, though she appreciated the help he was giving John.

In 1937 Margaret and John went to Nova Scotia and Cape Breton with recording equipment. They were amazed to find the songs and stories of the islanders still so fresh in the minds and the mouths of the people there, after three generations away. The songs were eventually transcribed and made into John's book *Songs Remembered in Exile*.

One day in April 1938, when Margaret was in hospital in Edinburgh, John suddenly announced that he had bought the island of Canna. His Oxford degree was in Rural Economy and he had always wanted to find a farm or, better still, an island which he could regenerate.

So here he was on Canna, with Margaret at his side, Canna is a small island of great beauty, wild flowers everywhere, unmolested wild-life, Gaelic-speaking people, everything they could have wished for.

There was much work to be done on the house, which had been neglected by previous owners. Margaret and a helper, Mary from Barra, set to with a will, scrubbing out the dairy, whitewashing, cleaning everything in sight.

In the fields, she amazed Big Hector, the grieve, by making stooks of corn, and by her skills at skinning rabbits and looking after orphan lambs – all things she had learnt to do during her days with Mairi and Peigí in South Uist.

The war years brought many difficulties. Travel to the mainland to sell cattle at market became most complicated, with permits having to be obtained as many areas were designated prohibited.

Her husband being away from time to time, Margaret was left in charge of the island, a situation which the head shepherd could not tolerate, though others were helpful and considerate. Wisely, she deferred to the knowledge and experience of these skilled men, till gradually they came to accept the fact that she, too, had skills, and could work along with them. So there she was, this tiny woman, with the slightly foreign voice, working her heart out on their island. Women had always, of course, been accustomed to take on the running of the croft when their men were away at the fishing, but this did not apply, perhaps, to the laird's wife!

Canna had become a sanctuary for people, birds, beasts and flowers. To use a gun was forbidden. One day, during the war, Margaret heard three rifle shots. She rushed down to the pier, where the eider ducks would sun themselves on the nearby skerries. Three fishing boats were tied up there. 'Who has the gun?' she yelled. 'Shooting the ducks is forbidden. I shall report you to the police.' She also said some other things, to the amazement and horror of a friend who had followed her. 'That's nothing', she retorted, implying there were worse swear-words to come.

She and John went out in the boat and lifted 11 dead eiders from the rocks. Margaret did report the matter and eventually the men were prosecuted for shooting deer on Rum.

After the war Canna became a refuge for people akin to the Campbells, poets and painters, musicians, scholars, naturalists, geologists. Archaeologists came too, but they were not allowed to disturb the Viking graves or the site of a Columban nunnery. Some small remains of early dwellings were excavated. Photographs and drawings were made of carved stones and crosses.

Margaret was kept busy entertaining all these guests, cooking for them, seeing to their needs. She was a superb hostess, kindly and welcoming, with spirited conversation and, of course, her lovely piano playing. The guests revelled in the library and in the evening ceilidhs of music and stories and song.

Margaret was fond of cats, having always had them as companions. When she married, Mairi had given her Wicked Willy, the Uist cat who came with her to Canna and whose descendants flourished there. She also bred Siamese cats and sold the kittens.

John had built up a pedigree herd of Highland cattle. The land was in good heart, the fencing and draining and organic manuring having played their part. As conservationists he and Margaret had seen to the protection of wildlife, planting trees and bushes to provide a habitat for butterflies and other creatures. Improvements were made to housing and to the pier. The Gaelic language also flourished on the island, the workers all native speakers from whom John collected many songs and stories.

In 1981 he decided to make Canna and the library over to the National Trust for Scotland. The library itself is a national treasure.

Twelve years later Margaret's book *From the Allegenies to the Hebrides* was published. It is a wonderful record of her early life in America and in parts of Europe and of the years she spent in South Uist, before coming to Canna, where she and John spent so many happy and productive years. The photographic illustrations greatly enhance the text.

In 1996, when on holiday in Italy with Margaret, staying in a nunnery near Fiesole, where there were Gaelic-speaking nuns,

John died. He was buried there, but after ten years his body was brought home for burial in Canna.

Margaret lived on in Canna House, with a Spanish woman librarian who was working on the massive collection of books.

As her centenary approached, a party from South Uist Historical Society sailed over to bring their good wishes, with pipe music and song. On one of her frequent visits to South Uist she had been delighted to hear some of the old songs she had written down still being sung by the young islanders. So her legacy lives on.

To mark her 100th birthday a television documentary on her life was made. She appeared on it, lively and articulate, playing her beloved piano. She lived on another year, then faded and was laid to rest in South Uist, beside her old friends Mairi and Peigí.

CHAPTER 21

Jemima Blackburn (1823–1909) – 'A Watercolourist of Perception'

IN THE 19TH CENTURY a Scots woman, Highland by adoption, began to record in exquisite watercolour the life and landscape, the birds and animals of her beloved country of Moidart. She was Jemima Blackburn.

'My birth was in sorrow and I think it left in me a gloomy and stormy disposition, more inclined to the pleasures of memory than those of hope'. So wrote Jemima Blackburn in the *Memoirs* she was persuaded to write during her later years. If her disposition was gloomy or stormy it did not prevent her from leading a most active and varied life and from becoming one of the most talented artists of the Victorian period.

She was born in 1823, in the newly-built house at 31 Heriot Row, Edinburgh, six months after the death of her father, James Wedderburn, who was Solicitor General for Scotland. Hence the sorrow. For the first ten years of her life she was delicate and often bed-ridden. It was then that she started to draw, as a means of therapy.

Friendship with the Blackburn family began when Jemima's brothers and the Blackburn boys were at school together at the Edinburgh Academy. Hugh Blackburn was two months younger than Jemima, a quiet, studious boy, with an interest in optics which led him to experiment with photography. Fascinated by these experiments, in which he tried to reproduce some of her drawings, Jemima began to test other means of reproduction of her work and taught herself to make woodcuts and wood engravings.

These efforts were perhaps what led her to realise that her drawing and painting was something more than a hobby.

When she was seventeen she was sent to London to stay with an aunt and uncle and a family of cousins. There she met many painters and other artists and was taken to the theatre and the opera. What she enjoyed perhaps most of all was a visit to the circus where she could study the movement of the horses and other animals. She herself was a most accomplished horsewoman and had trained horses at the country home of her mother's family, the Clerks of Penicuik.

After her return to Edinburgh and then the customary tour of Europe with members of the family, she settled down, in an attic studio, to draw. Her subjects were mostly the pets she had always kept – the dog, the cat, pigeons, even owls.

She was now twenty years old, getting restless and eager to extend her knowledge of the world of art. On a return visit to London in the winter of 1843 she was escorted by her cousin James, who took her to have tea with Landseer. The great painter was impressed by her drawings, particularly of animals, and arranged for a set of small watercolours illustrating the story of Tom Thumb, to be presented to the Queen's children. Landseer gave her a few informal lessons, the only actual training she ever received. She met many other famous people in London that year – Sir Robert Peel, Thackeray – and was invited to the Waterloo Ball by the Duke of Wellington.

By now Jemima was working seriously at her art. In 1846, Blackwoods, the Edinburgh publishers, brought out two books of fairy tales which she had illustrated. Two years later she had a painting, *Phaeton*, hung in the Royal Academy. Then her largest work – *Plough Horses startled by a Railway Engine* – was accepted and hung. She wrote to John Ruskin, whom she had met, asking his opinion of this picture. He replied with a long and carefully thought out piece of criticism and advice, declaring that she was 'capable of great things.' She was a versatile artist, painting in oils, etching, engraving, experimenting with photography, but her happiest medium is water colour.

In June of that year – 1849 – Jemima and Hugh Blackburn were married in St John's Chapel in Edinburgh. It was to be a long and happy marriage in which both partners were able to pursue their vocations and complementary interests. Hugh was a mathematician, being Professor of Mathematics at Glasgow University. He was also a keen botanist, geologist and ornithologist.

After a honeymoon spent walking in the Swiss Alps, they settled into life in the Old College in Glasgow, where the following year, their son William was born. He was named for his godfather William Thomson, Professor of Natural Philosophy at Glasgow, who was to become Lord Kelvin, a renowned scientist.

At this time the pre-Raphaelite movement was influencing poets, artists, designers and many others, including Jemima. It was part of the revolutionary and romantic spirit of the age, when creative minds were heeding Ruskin's words, 'Go to nature in all singleness of heart, selecting nothing, rejecting nothing.' In 1854 Jemima published *Illustrations from Scripture by an Animal Painter with Notes by a Naturalist*. It achieved immediate success and was praised by Landseer, Thackeray and Ruskin. She was also illustrating books by Charlotte Yonge and busily engaged in depicting scenes of wherever she happened to be. She designed a stained glass window for Glasgow Cathedral, in memory of her father. It is still there, in the Blackadder Aisle.

Every summer she, Hugh and the family had escaped the city to spend long, happy days in the country at a rented house in Ayrshire. They now decided that they must have a home of their own in the Highlands. In September 1854 they found the 'beautiful place' they were seeking – the estate of Roshven, in a remote part of the peninsula of Moidart, on the shore of Loch Ailort. They were to spend idyllic summers there, returning to Glasgow in winter.

By now two more children – Margaret and Hugh – had been born and Jemima depended much on the help of Barbara MacPhee, Babby, a motherly and affectionate person who looked after the children as well as the chickens, the ducks and other livestock and reigned supreme in the kitchen. Hugh had his hands full with plans for the rebuilding of the house, which was dilapidated, and for the management of the estate. The task was a huge one, with the building material having to be brought in by sea and workers hard to find. Despite all this, he made time to take long walks with the children and to go out fishing for mackerel in the evenings with Jemima.

She, meanwhile, was busy painting scenes of happy family life at Roshven – of a child's birthday party, of Hugh and William reading in the drawing-room, of a dance on the lawn, of Hugh and William Thomson working in the garden. She also began to paint the first of her many scenes of the life around her – of the people building a haystack, gathering bracken, shearing sheep, carting peats, waulking cloth, harvesting. The figures in these paintings are so full of life that the people depicted were able to recognise themselves immediately.

The Blackburns were well-liked by their tenantry. Hugh had new houses built for several of them; Jemima visited the sick, ignoring the risk of infection and supervising inoculations against smallpox. She bought groceries and clothing wholesale in Glasgow and sold the goods on at cost price from a 'shop' she set up in the attic. When many fishermen's boats were lost in a violent storm one winter she replaced them, using the money she made from her work.

They had many visitors to entertain at Roshven, including her cousin, James Clerk Maxwell, the celebrated scientist, whose theory of electro-magnetism is at the root of contemporary physics. Life was very full. Nevertheless she worked incessantly at her drawing and by 1862 had got together a collection of magnificent bird portraits which she called *Birds from Nature*. It was received with much enthusiasm. The *Scotsman* critic wrote: 'We have seen no such birds since Bewick's. We say this not ignorant of the magnificent plates by Selby, Audubon, Wilson and Gould.' She painted her birds from life, not from dead or stuffed specimens. This often involved what she called 'tubbing', floating in tubs across deep water, standing knee-deep in pools, climbing high cliffs to observe a buzzard's nest, painting an owl's young in a tall tree, from the rungs of a long ladder.

Soon after the publication of her *Birds* she accompanied her brother George on a journey to Egypt. He was suffering from tuberculosis and had been advised to find a warm climate for the winter. In the course of their visit they met the Prince of Wales and had many adventures. Then it was back home to entertain the many family friends.

Hospitality at Roshven was well-known. After dinner there would be much discussion of art and science, sometimes whist, and often music and dancing which went on into the small hours. Meanwhile Jemima, in her 42nd year, had given birth to another son, Alan. But her travelling days were not over. In 1874 she and Hugh had a three-month tour of Italy, during which she produced 162 paintings.

Two years later they travelled to Spain, Jemima finding time to paint almost as copiously. Then in 1878 she was invited to join a party, which included Anthony Trollope, to visit Iceland. Overcoming all hardships, they enjoyed the experience immensely.

With her usual extraordinary vitality Jemima produced 56 paintings in 15 days. Trollope, too, was a mighty producer and turned out 40 pages of 250 words a week. They enjoyed each other's company and on their return collaborated in an account of the trip.

By 1879 Hugh's hearing had become seriously impaired and he was obliged to resign his post at the University. Times were quiet, then, at Roshven. Nevertheless, he and Jemima continued to travel in Europe and into North Africa, at a leisurely pace, Jemima still painting. Her last major book – *Birds from Moidart* was published in 1895 and proved popular.

By then her influence was beginning to be felt by another artist – Beatrix Potter. For her tenth birthday Beatrix Potter had been given Blackburn's book of birds, drawn from nature, which she treasured. They met once, in London in 1891. Beatrix Potter describes Jemima in her journal as:

> A lady of apparently over 60, not tall, upright presence, and rather striking features. She spoke with a Scottish accent… She gave me the impression of a shrewd, practical woman able and accustomed to take the lead in managing a family estate.

Sadly, in her latter years Jemima's eyesight began to fail. Hugh persuaded her when they were both in their 80s, to write her memoirs. She did so, in a desultory fashion, he himself correcting and annotating her manuscript. At the age of 86 she died, Hugh surviving her by two months.

Her legacy to the world is in her paintings, which are themselves the product of her lively spirit at work in the fabulous beauty of her surroundings and with the constant support of her loving husband, her close-knit family and her many friends.

CHAPTER 22

Story-tellers of Our Time

IN EARLY TIMES Highland women expressed themselves – their loves, their sorrows, their feeling for the natural world of hill, sea, flower, bird – in poem and song. The richness of their magical language carried the gift of their imagination to the minds and memories of those around them. And this lived on through the generations.

What other forms of expression, what drawings, carvings, paintings, sculpted models may have been made perhaps in secret, then discarded, we may never know.

Women of the Highlands have always been keenly aware of, and in love with, their surroundings. This they were wont to express, along with their lore, in the magic of their native tongue, all safely stored in mind and heart, in poetry and in song. In these later days the word could be made to sing again, no longer in the language of the garden of Eden, in prose and in print, thus reaching into minds and hearts world-wide.

In one small crofting area in the hills to the north of Loch Ness – Abriachan – several women of the 20th century found the means of communicating verbally their vision of the world they saw around them.

What did they see? The shapes of the surrounding hills, the brilliant stars at night, storm-cloud, the first leaf buds on the birches, the wild geese winging in at dusk and the men and women working about the fields and houses, the children racing home from school.

Mairi MacDonald, whose mother belonged to Achcullin, in

Abriachan, her people having been pipers to the Grants of Seafield, and whose father came from nearby Glenmoriston, wrote *Highland Corranach*, the story of three generations of a Highland family, as progress and changes impinge on the traditional way of life. To quote from her foreword to the novel:

> I have tried to write this novel in the form of a corranach, the traditional lament of the Celt. I have named the parts after the different variations of the ancient piobaireachd (pibroch) and tried to keep the tempo of the various parts in line with the tempo of these variations. Words alone without a sense of music behind them mean so little to the Highlander. I hope it will help to explain some of our many troubles and some of our deep emotions. A Highland lament always ended on a note of hope.

The music of the pipes was in the life-blood of the MacDonalds of Achcullin. Mairi wrote about this music, and also wrote for many papers and journals and contributed papers to the Gaelic Society of Inverness. As a local historian, with a large library inherited from her father, she was always ready to share her vast store of knowledge with people who consulted her.

A contemporary of Mairi MacDonald – Eona Fraser – became a writer of great distinction. Her people were Frasers from Abriachan, though she herself was born in Inverness. Coming to visit, from an early age, with her father, she inherited a love of his birthplace which shines through in her imaginative stories in a collection called *The Hallowe'en Hero*. Here she tells of the way of life in a crofting community in the early 1900s, relating the happy times, the sad times, the fun, with glimpses of history and legend.

In one story, 'A window westwards' – she tells how her

grandfather, in a state of melancholy after being taken from his home at Druim, in Abriachan, to be cared for by the family in Inverness, was only restored to health when a window was opened in the west wall of the house to allow him a glimpse of his beloved country. Much of Eona's writing is as near poetry as prose can go. She married a minister Roy MacNicol and with him spent a considerable time in India, then in the Scottish borders, writing more books along the way. She came back to Abriachan whenever time allowed, to refresh her roots.

Another writer whose work came to be highly praised, Jessie Kesson, a MacDonald by birth, spent only a short time in Abriachan, but a time which was one of the most important in her life and which coloured much of her subsequent writing.

She came, as a young woman, to live with a crofting family high in the hills, at Achbuie, after suffering illness as a result of spending years in an orphanage. Here, she recovered her health in the clean air and married another orphan, John Kesson, boarded in another croft.

They lived for many years as farm workers and eventually moved to London, where Jessie found work of various kinds. Soon, her writing took off. In one early piece, written for radio – *The Red Rock* – Abriachan is instantly recognisable, the beautiful red granite cliffs the setting for a sad tale.

Her books – *The White Bird Passes*, *Glitter of Mica*, *Another Time, Another Place* tell of life further east, in Morayshire, or in the Black Isle, but she always kept her love of the Highlands. In a collection of short stories – *Where the Apple Ripens* – one, *Road of No Return*, tells of coming back to her adopted country and the memories it evoked. Her work is highly acclaimed nationwide.

At her own request her ashes were scattered at the Red Rock, in Abriachan.

In the 1950s Maureen MacIlwrath, with her husband and small son, came to live for a time in Abriachan. She was enchanted with the place, came to know the people, the way of life, the stories. She would walk about, talking to the people, looking at things.

The result was a book – *The Kelpie's Pearls*, written under the pen-name Mollie Hunter. It is pure magic, magic on the doorstep. The setting can be clearly identified and is shown to children who still come to see the pool where the kelpie lived.

Mollie Hunter's later historical novels, which brought her world-wide fame, were Highland-based and she was never far in thought from her beloved hill-top place. *The Kelpie's Pearls* soon became a children's classic. As a folk-tale of today, long may it be read by children and children's children everywhere.

CHAPTER 23

Exodus

AFTER THE PASSING OF the Education Act of 1872 which made schooling compulsory up to the age of 13, girls in the Highlands found themselves able and willing to pursue further studies and to look towards the professions.

Nursing and teaching seemed to offer opportunities. They had always been used to coping with illness, accident, death, in their own or their neighbours' homes. Putting on a white cap and apron made little difference. They could at all times be depended on to care devotedly, to act wisely, to keep cool. Their work as nurses took them to many strange towns and cities where they had to cope with loneliness and anxiety. Their parents were not used to writing letters and lack of home news was often distressing. But many of them learned English and obtained qualifications that took them on in the profession. They had no competition with men. Some of them married doctors. Some went overseas to work in missionary establishments. Their reputation world-wide was great.

Girls who were used to helping younger brothers and sisters with 'lessons', they were the ones whose own love of learning took them on to share it with those in the class-room, perhaps first of all as a 'pupil-teacher' in their own school. As their confidence grew they could progress to training college and so to a school in a nearby, or distant, town. Here, like their friends in nursing, they had to suffer times of loneliness and distress among strange company, with strange ways. But many made it to the higher echelons. Young teachers and nurses alike would return home whenever some free time came round. Home was always the dearest place.

Girls who had not pursued their school studies were also finding work in the developing towns and cities during the 19th and 20th centuries. In Aberdeen the textile industry offered opportunities for those accustomed to working with fabrics. In Dundee the jute mills needed many workers, particularly those with weaving skills. The noise and bustle of this work affected the hearing and the general health of many young women, but the pay was welcome. Some married and stayed on in Dundee.

Towards the end of the 19th century, when the universities began to accept women students, girls from the Highlands responded eagerly. Highland schools such as Inverness Royal Academy, Dingwall Academy and Kingussie High School produced students of high calibre.

With their habits of hard work many women succeeded in establishing themselves in the higher ranks of the professions, especially in medicine. Their earning tended to be less than that of their male counterparts and some were looked on with glances of suspicion. However, they gradually made their way to normal acceptance.

Then came the wars. The Boer War of the late 19th–early 20th century took many fighting men away to South Africa, the Highland regiments, including the locally raised Lovat Scouts, being particularly involved. Some men must have wondered what they were doing there, farmers fighting farmers?

During the Great War of 1914–1918, women took over men's jobs of various kinds – working in munitions factories, driving ambulances, manning look-outs. Women of the Highlands were among them. Pushed to the extremes of their ability and their strength, they gained confidence in themselves, partnering the men.

In the Second World War women were even more fully

engaged in the turmoil of the time. Many of them joined the armed forces, opting for service in the navy, as 'wrens' in particular. They also worked on the land and in the forests.

Highland survivors of the conflicts were disappointed that the 'land fit for heroes' did not materialise on their return. Some tried, unsuccessfully, to grab a share. Women were left to care for disabled husbands and sons while coping with the stringency of the time.

Gradually things began to settle down. Developments which had been postponed while the fighting raged came slowly to fruition. These developments were to transform the lives of women in the Highlands.

When hill tracks became roads fit for the wheels of gig or even motor-car, scattered family members could more easily keep in touch. Water coming from a tap saved carrying pails to and from the well, though the elderly still preferred a drink that hadn't come 'through the iron' but straight from the spring. Telephone boxes began to appear. That little bright red cabin down the road was a welcome sight in times of urgent need.

The greatest asset of all, of course, was the advent of hydro-electric power. To light the kitchen at the flick of a switch, to warm the house at another, certainly seemed like a miracle. Oil-lamps and hot water piggies could be discarded as the pylons marched across the hills.

Portable gas could power a small heater and a cooking point but the 'electric' had a magic of its own. Soon the 'wireless' could be plugged in, batteries were no longer needed, and then came the television. When the first set arrived a new kind of 'ceilidh' began to happen – people gathered wide-eyed round the 'box' to gaup in disbelief at the antics on the tiny screen. This did open up a new world, but it was an unreal world, most of it, and was soon to lose its initial appeal. A good-going shinty match with bumps and bruises galore for the girls to admire and a hearty song on the way home was still the favoured entertainment for the young.

The women had little time to watch the 'box' but they did avidly scan the shiny pages of the catalogues the postie brought and were soon putting aside whatever could be spared for the purchase of an electric iron and, later, a washing-machine. No more impossibly heavy smoothing irons filled with hot embers, no more wash-boards that took the skin off your fingers – it seemed like a foretaste of paradise!

And there would then be time, that most precious commodity, time to spare, time to do an extra baking for an elderly neighbour, time to plant up the garden, even time to walk to the bus for a trip to town. Possibilities began to grow at an alarming rate. Alarming was indeed the word, for, with all that crazy song and dance now on the screen in the kitchen, the young began to feel that they were, perhaps, missing something after all.

So an exodus began. Mothers had to see sons and daughters off to that dizzy world knowing, in their hearts, that a return would be difficult. Perhaps when they were older and had seen enough...

CHAPTER 24

Isabel Frances Grant (1887–1983) – Collector Extraordinaire

YET ANOTHER MEMBER of the Grant family who made a great and unique contribution to the story of Highland life and culture was Isabel Frances (known as Elsie), who lived from 1887 to 1983.

She was born in Edinburgh, the eldest of the six children of Colonel Grant of the Seaforth Highlanders and Isobel MacKintosh of Balnespick in Strathdearn. When she was quite young her parents went to India, leaving her in the care of her grandfather, Sir Patrick Grant, who was governor of Chelsea Hospital in London, and a spinster aunt. Several governesses saw to her education. She was often taken to the British Museum, where she admired the Elgin Marbles and found them a great source of inspiration, opening up the wonders of the ancient world.

During the First World War Elsie worked in London at the Ministry of Labour, as research assistant to Sir Henry Clay and to Maynard Keynes. This enabled her to develop scholarly and critical faculties which she was to use to great effect in later life. After the war she was able to travel, going to Stockholm, Oslo and Amsterdam. In these countries she found open-air museums showing what was termed 'peasant' culture. It was here that she had a vision of what a museum of the Highlands could be. The Gaelic way of life was, she maintained, a survival of an ancient aristocratic culture, not primitive or 'peasant'. By preserving the material culture of the Highland people, their traditions and values could be highlighted.

The springboard for the realisation of her idea was the success of the Highland Exhibition held in Inverness in 1930. Elsie, with her formidable energy and determination, was largely responsible for the setting-up of this remarkable display of artefacts – household goods, implements, fabrics, weapons, documents – from all over the Highlands and beyond. The response from contributors was tremendous. More than 2,000 items had been gathered, some of inestimable, unique interest.

In her speech at the opening ceremony she emphasised the importance of keeping a record of the past. By preserving the homely objects in everyday use by the people of the Highlands, their whole way of life, she pointed out, their customs, traditions, beliefs could become real again. In her mind was the hope that some of the objects in the exhibition might form the basis of the Highland museum she longed to create. A few did find their way into her custody, most were returned to their owners.

Inspired by the interest shown in this exhibition, which had attracted over 2,000 visitors in two months, Elsie Grant set about looking for a place where the things she had managed to gather could be shown.

In 1934, with the help of a small legacy from her much-loved aunt, she bought a disused United Free Church on the island of Iona. This was an attractive place but proved to be somewhat inaccessible for visitors. After three years she found space on the mainland, in an old church at Laggan on Speyside. This meant a precarious removal of her precious collection and proved to be only a respite as, with the outbreak of war imminent, the building was threatened with requisition.

She looked around desperately for somewhere to house the growing collection and finally found Pitmain Lodge, a Georgian shooting lodge, with three acres of ground, near the railway station in Kingussie. This was really the answer to her quest.

In Pitmain Lodge, there was a houseful of rooms where items

could be displayed in different categories. There was also accommodation for herself and for her housekeeper, Mrs Myra Grant, the daughter of a Skye crofter. This lady was of the greatest help in looking after the museum as well as the house and livestock in the grounds. Apart from some part-time helpers from the village, she was the only assistant to the curator. But everything soon took shape. The walls were covered with notes about the uses of the things displayed, with proverbs, or the words of songs. Elsie Grant had always been interested in this educational aspect of the collection. So much knowledge of peoples' ancestors and their way of life had been lost.

On 1 June 1944 the place now known as 'Am Fasgadh', The Shelter, was opened to the public. It was run by Elsie herself, at her own expense, with little public support, though Mr Petty of Kingussie and Sheriff Grant and his wife were good friends of the museum. No charge was made for entry. A collection box was placed at the door.

Meanwhile, whenever she could get away, leaving her few helpers in charge, Elsie Grant travelled the country-side by car, often ending up on foot, looking for treasures. With the end of the war and the 'no-go' areas opened up again, she was able to get far afield and to the islands, where she knew many lovely old artefacts still remained. She managed to rescue quite a few of them, some even from rubbish dumps where they had been discarded as old-fashioned.

She did not always enjoy collecting. Though she was tall and of commanding presence, she said of herself, 'I am shy and lacking in self-confidence and social address'. Fearful of intruding on privacy, and understanding her Highland people as she did, she was able, occasionally, to offer a little money, where she could see it might be welcome, for some special object.

In her travels she was helped by many friends. Mrs MacDougall of MacDougall, a keen antiquarian, with whom she stayed, got a crofter to sell her a 'chimney', a 'hanging lum', which she managed to dismantle and transport to Kingussie.

Mr and Mrs Seton Gordon, with their knowledge of people and places in their part of Skye, at Duntulm, were also most helpful.

Journeying in the islands, by boat, also gave her a freshened perspective, what she called 'an added faculty for sensing the reality of the past... that it actually happened to people like oneself upon tangible earth and water and that its effects are like strands of varying thicknesses woven into the fabric of our present-day life.'

Back at Am Fasgadh she got four buildings put up in the grounds – an old 'black house', built in traditional island style by a crofter, one of Inverness-shire style, one mason-built, of more modern design, and a 'clach-mill', a Norse-type small mill with original horizontal stones. Women dressed traditionally, did their spinning, milked a cow, baked oatcakes on a peat fire. Sometimes they sang at their work. This was what Elsie Grant wanted to show – the work practices and the artistic element combined.

During this time her writings began to appear. She had already published *Everyday Life on an Old Highland Farm, 1769–1787*, based on the account books of a farm in her mother's family, that of William MacKintosh of Balnespick in Badenoch, and in 1935, *The Lordship of the Isles*. In the 1950s she published *The Clan Donald*, *The Clan Grant* and *The MacLeods*. Then, in 1966, appeared her *Highland Folkways*, a very full and appropriately illustrated book which became a bible for all those interested in the story of the Highlands and the Highland people. In that year she was asked to give the Rhind lectures by the Society of Antiquaries, an honour which she greatly appreciated.

Altogether she wrote over a dozen books as well as articles in various journals. In 1948, in recognition of the value of her work, she received an honorary Lld. from Edinburgh University. This also pleased her, conscious as she was of being entirely self-educated. In the Laureation Address reference was made to her scholarly publications and also to the collection at 'Am Fasgadh' – the largest of its kind in Scotland, which she 'created single-handed from her own resources'. The address concluded 'services such as these merit a doctor's gown'.

By this time the collection had grown so large and so all-encompassing, with people contributing items on a generous scale, that Dr Grant began to feel anxious about its future. The years of responsibility and of active involvement in the project were beginning to take their toll.

It was decided to seek help from the Pilgrim Trust, a body set up to assist enterprises of historic interest such as Am Fasgadh. A grant was duly made. This enabled Dr Grant in 1954, with the valued help of Professor Taylor, principal of Aberdeen University, to make over the care of the collection to the four Scottish Universities. A grant was obtained from the Society of Antiquaries for the compilation of a catalogue, a much valued asset.

In 1959, aged 72, Dr Grant received another honour – the MBE. With the future of the museum assured, she was then able to seek some leisure in her flat in Edinburgh. Here she was pleased to offer hospitality to many people interested in Highland culture, especially to students and scholars. She continued to write articles for newspapers and journals. Dr Grant died in 1983. Her ashes are interred in that lovely, lonely graveyard at Dalarossie in Strathdearn.

Were she alive today she would surely scarcely believe how her original idea for a folk museum had blossomed. Am Fasgadh was run for a time by the District Council, with volunteer help. Then the County Council took over, and now the Highland Council is in charge, with a fully qualified staff. A huge new development at nearby Newtonmore is taking shape.

This development would have greatly pleased 'herself', for it is a whole reconstructed township. There are houses of various types – some of turf and wattle, some of stone, some with heather thatch and central fire-place. Stone was brought from a deserted settlement in a nearby glen. There is a kiln and a saw-mill, dry-stone dykes, and some crops have been sown. Lately a school and a church have been brought in and set up, with original furnishings, pews, desks and equipment.

Demonstrations of various crafts take place regularly – spinning, weaving, dyeing, rope-making, and peat-cutting, thatching, wattling, scything; all the activities that were part of the old way of life. Visitors are invited to join in and try their skills. Traditional music, song and dance are there, too. And livestock of various kinds busily pursue their own interests. Along with Am Fasgadh, this is a living, moving memorial to a woman of outstanding vision and dedication – Dr Isabel Frances Grant.

CHAPTER 25

These Days

WOMEN OF THE HIGHLANDS and the Islands are, of course, part of the huge village that encompasses the globe. Those who have qualified as professionals may have wandered to far parts, far cities, working as teachers, doctors, nurses, lawyers.

Wherever they go they take their inherited values with them, their integrity, their ingrained habit of hard work and their wish to be of service to others. And they take their song and dance with them to the most far-flung places, too. Who else could have taught the people of Borneo to step-dance their way to happiness, the girls of Peru to sing 'Mairi's Wedding', and tired workers in Glasgow to ceilidh the night away?

Those qualified women who prefer to stay nearer home may practice their skills in or near the vicinity of their birth. Their understanding of the way of life of those they attend helps them in the advice and treatment they can offer.

Women living even in fairly remote areas can access government or other funding to set themselves up in small outlets for craft work in which many of them are skilled – weaving, knitting, patchwork, quilting.

Alternatively, they can cater for the ever-increasing demand for organic produce by growing fruit and vegetables in poly-tunnels or well-sheltered greenhouses.

With pure air and pure water in abundance, produce grown naturally is also attractive to those looking for food that is really fresh. Hotels, lodges, holiday homes all have customers ready and eager to buy in the not-so-distant neighbourhood. Improved roads and transport facilities – buses and vans – make the distribution of foodstuffs easier than in the past.

Telecommunication also allows women to do office work from home. A small corner of the kitchen will suffice as a work base, when husbands are out at work, perhaps children at school. In the summer an outbuilding or shed can be used.

With the young women working happily in an area the young men are encouraged to stay, those improved transport facilities enabling them to find paid work, even at some distance. So there will be social life, families will grow, the school will stay open, perhaps the Post Office, even a small shop. There will be communities again.

Incomers will be made welcome as they contribute their own gifts, perhaps new skills, and bring their experience of the wider world to enliven intercourse with the people native to the district.

As confidence in the strength of the community grows, with the satisfaction of establishing a way of life again and also of keeping contact with the world beyond the horizon, women may look to making their voices heard in local affairs and in those of nation-wide importance. 'Caring' is perhaps the key word here, as it always was, caring for the ill, the elderly, the deprived, and also for the environment. They find themselves on committees, on councils, in Parliament, on bodies of all kinds, using their most expressive arguments as they lead the discussions on the bettering of conditions for everyone.

In fund-raising, an important part of all such activity, women are particularly adept at catching the hearts and loosening the purse-strings. And the hours worked are countless, as they have always been. Nevertheless, a song is never far away.

From the earliest times, it was the women who made the far lands sing. Life was hard, sometimes sad, but that was accepted and you made a song on it, a happy song for love, a slow song for parting. The busiest wife and mother found time to plant a pansy under the window, or a white rose climbing by the door. This was a way of singing, too.

Today's singers – Karen Matheson with 'the voice of an angel', Mary Ann Kennedy who also composes, Fiona MacKenzie, the Màiri Mhór Fellow – these and many others keep the Gaelic language alive with their singing.

Other women bring the language and the traditional way of life of which it was always a part, into people's ken – Margaret Bennett as a historian and a singer of Gaelic songs, Margaret MacKay and her colleagues at the School of Scottish Studies in Edinburgh.

Work is so much less heavy now, with modern inventions. The creel no longer has to be carried, the slype pulled, the quern turned or the sickle slashed. Backs, shoulders and arms have respite. Women can enjoy their work and the results are sometimes astonishing. What sings as sweetly as a many-coloured quilting, or a handful of grapes?

And the women who produced them will be dancing till cock-crow or sitting in a council chamber discussing the latest development in green energy.

It's all there in the Highlands – the singing and the gold!

Bibliography

Baird, Rosemary: *Mistress of the House, Great Ladies and Grand Houses 1670–1830*, Weidenfield and Nicolson, London, 2003

Barron, Roderick: *A Highland Lady of Letters, Mrs Grant of Laggan*, Transactions of the Gaelic Society of Inverness, vol. 42, Inverness, 1954

Bassin, Ethel: *Frances Tolmie 1840–1920 and her Circle, The Old Songs of Skye*, Routledge and Kegan Paul, London, 1977

Bennett, Margaret: *Scottish Customs from the Cradle to the Grave*, Birlinn, Edinburgh, 2004

Carmichael, Alexander: *Carmina Gadelica*, Scottish Academic Press, Edinburgh, 1976

Cheape, Hugh: 'Dr I F Grant (1887–1983) the Highland Folk Museum and a Bibliography of her written works', *Review of Scottish Culture*, no 2, 1986

Craig, Maggie: *Damn' Rebel Bitches, the Women of the '45*, Mainstream Publishing, Edinburgh, 1997

Dillon Myles and Chadwick, Nora: *The Celtic Realms*, Weidenfield and Nicolson, London, 1967

Douglas, Hugh: *Flora MacDonald, the most loyal rebel*, Alan Sutton, Stroud, 1993

Ellis, Peter Beresford: *Celtic Women, Women in Celtic Society and Literature*, Constable, London, 1995

Celtic Inheritance, Frederick Muller, London, 1985

Fairley, Rob (editor): *Jemima, the Paintings and Memoirs of a Victorian Lady*, Canongate, Edinburgh, 1988

Fyfe, J G: *Scottish Diaries and Memoirs*, Eneas MacKay, Stirling, 1942

Grant, Anne: *Letters from the Mountains*, Longman, London, 1806

Grant, Elizabeth of Rothiemurchus: *Memoirs of a Highland Lady, 1797–1855*, John Murray, London, 1967

A Highland Lady in France, 1843–1845, Tuckwell Press, E. Linton, 1996

A Highland Lady in Ireland, Canongate Classics, Edinburgh, 1991

Grant, I F: *Highland Folkways*, Routledge and Kegan Paul, London, 1961

Livingston, Sheila: *Scottish Customs*, Birlinn, Edinburgh, 2000

MacKenzie, Alexander: *The Isle of Skye in 1882–1883*, A & W MacKenzie, Inverness, 1883

MacPherson, Mary: *Poems and Songs*, Inverness, 1891

Nicolson, Alexander: *History of Skye*, Skye, 1930

Ross, Anne: *Folklore of the Scottish Highlands,* Tempus Publications Ltd, Stroud, 2000

Sanderson, Margaret H B: *A Kindly Place*, Tuckwell Press, East Linton, 2002

Shaw, Margaret Fay: *From the Alleghenies to the Hebrides*, Canongate Press Ltd, Edinburgh, 1993

Smout, T C and Lambert, R A (editors): *Rothiemurchus*, Scottish Cultural Press, 1999

Sutherland, Elizabeth: *Five Euphemias*, Constable, London, 1999

Thompson, F: *The Supernatural Highlands*, Luath Press Ltd, Edinburgh, 1997

Transactions of the Gaelic Society of Inverness: Inverness, 1871–2005

Withers, C W J: *Urban Highlanders*, Tuckwell Press, E. Linton, 1998

Glossary

Carlin – man, fellow
Ceilidh – (n) a social gathering, with singing, story-telling and dancing
Clarsach – Highland harp
Coronach – song to the dead
Croon – (n) slow, quiet song
Crotal – a yellow lichen
Cruisie – an old form of oil lamp
Girdle or *griddle* – flat pan
Green – short grass
Guddle – catch fish by hand, lit. trick
Herd – (n) man or boy herding sheep or cattle
Lilt – (n) melodious song
Machair – coastal meadowland
Quern – hand-mill for grinding corn
Reitach – form of betrothal
Shieling – summer pasture
Slype – hand-pulled sledge
Smoor – bank the fire with ash
Spirtle – stick for stirring porridge
Wattling – lining for walls made of wattle

Index

Some other books published by **LUATH** PRESS

Cattle on a Thousand Hills: Farming Culture in the Highlands of Scotland

Katharine Stewart
ISBN: 978-1906817-44-2 PBK £7.99

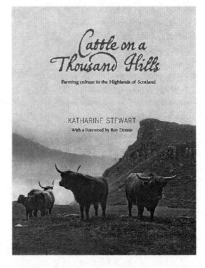

One cold spring morning I had a lovely surprise. As the first drops of milk spurted into the pail a blackbird, who had taken up residence in the byre over the winter, began to sing his little inward song, in rehearsal for the full-throated version he would sing from the branch of the rowan later on. This was a moment of delight which will be with me always.

KATHARINE STEWART

While their role has been all too often overlooked by historians, cattle have played an integral part in the economy, ecology and culture of Highland life. Although many of these animals and their keepers have been abandoned in favour of sheep walks and deer forests, their legacy has remained through stories, paintings and songs.

Infused by the author's own experiences of small-holding at 'the end of the crofting era', this book offers an excellent insight into the social history and colourful customs associated with tending cattle on crofts, on shielings and on the drove roads of old, in an account that is populated by legendary figures, mighty beasts and characters larger than life.

Perhaps most importantly of all, however, this is a history that looks to the future – a recent revival in cattle and traditional practices could pave the way for the truly sustainable agricultural practices so crucial to the fate of the planet at large.

The Story of Loch Ness

Katharine Stewart
ISBN 978-1905222-77-3 PBK £7.99

Known throughout the world for its legendary inhabitant, Loch Ness has inspired folklore and fascination in the hearts of those who visit it for centuries. But what of the characters, the history and the myths which enchanted inhabitants and travellers alike long before the first sightings of the so-called Loch Ness Monster? Katharine Stewart takes us on a journey through the past and the politics, the heroes and villains, and the natural beauties that are the true source of the magic of Loch Ness.

Where did the name Loch Ness come from, and how did Cherry Island come to be? What can be said of the wildlife that makes its home around the loch? Who determined the fate of the Loch Ness valley as we know it today?

While the depths and secrets of Loch Ness may never be revealed entirely, Stewart provides the answers to these and so many other questions in this compelling guide to one of Scotland's most famous places.

The Story of Loch Ness
With a Foreword by T.C. Smout
KATHARINE STEWART

From geological origins to connections with the industrial revolution and speculation on the future of this national treasure, she presents a rich tapestry of unforgettable anecdotes.
SCOTLAND IN TRUST

... a treasure trove of information about the loch and everything round it in very readable form. Don't miss it.
Rob Scott THE SUNDAY POST

Luath Press Limited

committed to publishing well written books worth reading

LUATH PRESS takes its name from Robert Burns, whose little collie Luath (*Gael.,* swift or nimble) tripped up Jean Armour at a wedding and gave him the chance to speak to the woman who was to be his wife and the abiding love of his life. Burns called one of 'The Twa Dogs' Luath after Cuchullin's hunting dog in Ossian's *Fingal*. Luath Press was established in 1981 in the heart of Burns country, and now resides a few steps up the road from Burns' first lodgings on Edinburgh's Royal Mile.

Luath offers you distinctive writing with a hint of unexpected pleasures.

Most bookshops in the UK, the US, Canada, Australia, New Zealand and parts of Europe either carry our books in stock or can order them for you. To order direct from us, please send a £sterling cheque, postal order, international money order or your credit card details (number, address of cardholder and expiry date) to us at the address below. Please add post and packing as follows: UK – £1.00 per delivery address; overseas surface mail – £2.50 per delivery address; overseas airmail – £3.50 for the first book to each delivery address, plus £1.00 for each additional book by airmail to the same address. If your order is a gift, we will happily enclose your card or message at no extra charge.

Luath Press Limited
543/2 Castlehill
The Royal Mile
Edinburgh EH1 2ND
Scotland
Telephone: 0131 225 4326 (24 hours)
Fax: 0131 225 4324
email: sales@luath.co.uk
Website: www.luath.co.uk